CLIMBING MOUNTAINS IN

Stilettos

NOT YOUR AVERAGE
TRAIL GUIDE TO LIFE

ANN TINKHAM AND CAROL BRUNELLI

SOURCEBOOKS, INC.®
NAPERVILLE, ILLINOIS

This publication is designed to provide accurate and authoritative information in regard to the subject matter covered. It is sold with the under-
standing that the publisher is not engaged in rendering legal, accounting,
or other professional service. If legal advice or other expert assistance is
required, the services of a competent professional person should be
sought.—*From a Declaration of Principles Jointly Adopted by a Committee of the American Bar Association and a Committee of Publishers and
Associations*

Published by Sourcebooks, Inc.
P.O. Box 4410, Naperville, Illinois 60567-4410
(630) 961-3900
Fax: (630) 961-2168
www.sourcebooks.com

Printed and bound in the United States of America.
VP 10 9 8 7 6 5 4 3 2 1

CONTENTS

DEDICATION

To raising up all women in this world.
The more women who get to the summit,
the stronger we will be.

ACKNOWLEDGMENTS

Ann Tinkham

To Carol, for keeping the creative spark for this project alive and for being a master of improvisational collaboration.

To James and Katelyn, for being my inspiration and for the tomato on a toothpick.

To Jay, for being my angel, cherished friend, lawyer, accountant, handyman, and car guy.

To Z for extracting and cherishing the bean.

To Kathy and Mary, for being my soul sisters.

To Jala, for the weekly giggles, girl talk, and Big D kvetching.

To my dad, who taught me that if you can dream it, you can do it.

To my mom, who showed me that being true to oneself is the only path worth taking.

To Amy, who taught me about the rewards that bad girls reap.

To my uncle Charlie, who shared my love of word-smithing.

To my writers' group, Witches and Wenches, who infuse me with all things writerly.

To Jim and Barbara, who tend to my chi and spirit to keep the muse alive.

To Liz, Dawn, and the group, for helping me keep my head on straight.

To Judy, who showed us what a true mentor is.

To Lisa, who believed in our project, and to Bethany, an insightful, creative editor and true collaborator. To Shana and Ewurama, who picked up the baton and sprinted to the finish with us.

To Barbara, who snapped our glamour shot on the rocks.

Thanks to Viviane, Kathy, Barb, Ann, Elizabeth, Randy, and Gerry for their sassy comebacks. Carol and I have some sassy friends!

Carol Brunelli

First of all, thank you, Ann, for writing this book with me. You're a great partner in collaboration and an even better friend. Tons of love and gratitude for my friends in Boulder, Boston, and at the Boulder College of Massage Therapy for their encouragement and enthusiasm for this project. To the Juju girls for testing out our material when it was in its infancy. A special thanks to photographer Robbie Steinbach for orchestrating our first ever photo shoot along the banks of the Rio Grande. Thank you to Jessica and BJ of Clear Pixel Design for their generosity and for our gorgeous website. I am ever so grateful to my love, Bill, and my family for loving me and giving me some great stories to tell. And I am eternally indebted to my mother, Margo, for her backbone, sass, and unwavering spirit. You taught me well.

Prologue

Invoke your inner stiletto.
—Miss Meghan

You're probably wondering why this book is titled *Climbing Mountains in Stilettos*. You may be thinking, Excuse me, but stilettos aren't the best footwear selection for hiking. Yeah, we know. Ann hikes in trail running shoes and Carol in hybrid trail shoes. You wouldn't catch us dead hiking in stilettos. Or if we did, we might find ourselves ankle deep in mud or snow.

You may then ask: So, is this book offering impractical advice for women? Not at all. We believe that climbing mountains in stilettos is a metaphor for being a strong female in our culture. To summit in stilettos requires balance, grace, strategy, audacity, spirit, strength, and determination. And think about it—if you can climb a mountain in stilettos, you can accomplish just about anything.

Consider this: As you navigate through your life, do you sometimes feel unsteady, off balance, and vulnerable? Do you also sometimes feel sexy, powerful, stylish, and feminine? This is where stilettos come in.

The origin of the word *stilettos* comes from the switchblade—a kind of knife used by pirates, gangsters, and other bad boys and girls (yes, there were some female pirates). A stiletto is a long, narrow-bladed dagger. The stiletto gained popularity during the Renaissance when it was used as a weapon against armored knights. The thin blade could slip through gaps in a knight's armor, delivering a fatal wound.

A stiletto heel is tall and thin, appearing as if a dagger is affixed to the bottom of the shoe. Some believe these shoes are as powerful as the stiletto blade. The pointed-toe stiletto heel that was the symbol of female oppression in the 1960s is now associated with powerful women who are climbing the upper tiers of the corporate ladder.

Much to the dismay of some forty- and fifty-something practical-shoe-wearing feminists, it is the stiletto-clad career women who are relishing the hard-won benefits of the feminist era. They are blending femininity with audacity to get ahead. These ambitious women on Wall Street and in the City district of London are called Spike-Heeled Power Bitches. (Sounds a lot better than Orthopedic Power Bitches. Doesn't it?)

Whoever said that empowered women had to wear sensible shoes? The important point here is that we can't judge a woman by her shoes, now can we? Let's shatter stereotypes and consider the possibility of a come-hither femme fatale in Birkenstocks, a nun in combat boots, Wonder Woman in UGGs, or a Supreme Court justice in stilettos.

Many women attest to the power of the stiletto heel, claiming that it boosts their confidence and feelings of invincibility in business meetings—their distractive arousing qualities triggering sexual desires in businessmen. Which is more enticing: a business woman in stilettos or a PowerPoint presentation with colorful pie charts? As men are fighting off their fantasies, women can take control and win arguments or secure deals. (Think female spies in James Bond flicks.)

The stiletto has been popular for half a decade—a symbol of femininity and sexuality. From Marilyn Monroe and Jayne Mansfield in the 1950s to Sarah Jessica Parker in the early 2000s, these high heels have enjoyed a long run of popularity.

Women who wear these shoes feel elegant, fashionable, and empowered, even though balancing in them can be tricky. Walking over steel grates and other obstacles in the urban landscape can be downright perilous. As precarious as they may be, these spiked heels can morph into a lethal weapon in two seconds flat. Vulnerability translated into power.

But having power and using it are two different things. One of the biggest problems that women face is being ambivalent about their own power. We should be comfortable with the idea of wielding power. We mustn't feel that it detracts from our femininity. This is like taking the chocolate out of a chocolate bar. What do you have left? Only the sugar.

Historically, femininity and power have been dichotomized. You're either feminine and sexy or powerful, but not both. There's power in femininity and there's femininity in power.

Climbing Mountains in Stilettos distills this potent mix in the form of a trail guide. All the trails in this book lead to Stilettos Summit, a place where your fully empowered self resides, a place that represents your peak potential. To get you to the top, we've mapped out strategies for mastering life's trails and travails. Reaching Stilettos Summit requires dancing on Razor's Edge, breaking the trail on Pioneer Pass, stalking up Mountain Lion Pass, and soaking up

Luscious Body Hot Springs. It requires skipping down the Yellow Brick Road, leaping over Sabotage Gulch, mastering the Double Black Diamond Challenge, scaling the Sassy Comeback Arch, and maneuvering Bushwhackers' Gorge.

Although we can't summit for you, we *can* share a secret. Summiting requires invoking your inner stiletto. How do you do this? The way a bad girl does—by imagining she is a super heroine in spiked power heels, with super powers that allow for flawless navigation, early detection of threats, and the ability to cut through fear with a stiletto blade. She sees herself in her stilettos ready to conquer the forces that threaten to knock her off the trail to Stilettos Summit, whether they are the lure of Miss Goody Two Shoes, the slings and arrows of jealous wood sprites, or a wrong turn leading down a slippery slope.

It's now time to invoke your inner stiletto and hit the trail. But for "goddess" sake, don't *actually* climb a mountain in stilettos. However, if you're daring enough to take on the stiletto challenge, send us a photo of you in your stilettos at the summit, and you'll be featured in our next book. We promise.

Razor's Edge

I wrote the story myself. It's about a girl who lost
her reputation and never missed it.
—Mae West

About This Trail: This trail is not for the faint of
heart. Imagine walking on Razor's Edge with sheer
drops on either side. Keep your feet on the trail and
reach for the stars. Too few women have dared to
tread here before.

Duration: Hopefully, it won't take you a lifetime. If
it does, you'll be reincarnated as a sherpa.

Distance: It depends how much convincing you're
going to need. If you score a four or below on the

quiz at the end of the chapter, you'll need to climb out of a crevasse just to get on the trail.

Difficulty: On a scale from one to ten, it's an eleven. This trail begins as a moderate ascent, but then tapers off into narrow steep trail with two thousand-foot drops on either side. It requires enlightenment and guts.

Elevation: Take some deep breaths (and maybe even an oxygen tank) before you hit this trail. It's a steep climb, but the higher you climb, the less help you're going to need.

Backpack Essentials: Ovaries, a leather cat suit, vision, nerves of steel, and fine china for breaking.

What to Leave Behind: Good girl rules, things your mother taught you, people who hold you back, double standards, and fear of heights.

Early Pitfalls: The trail becomes as thin as a razor's edge and as steep as a double black diamond ski slope, so you'll need to proceed slowly. Don't get frustrated with your pace. Also, watch out for people who think that women have already come far enough and persuade you to go back where you came from.

Trail Tip: Steer clear of good girls and good-old boys, who are poised to impede your progress every step of the way. Don't look down or back; you may freeze in your tracks from vertigo and spaghetti legs. Watch your footwork; one wrong step could send you plunging into the abyss.

At the Trail's End: Leave the good girl rules behind to discover your bad girl self. On this trail you'll learn that the things you were taught about being a good girl are bad and the things you learned about being a bad girl are good.

If you're like many women, you have lived your life following good girl rules, running after elusive fantasies, and living up to unrealistic expectations. You've been pleasing and accommodating, sexy but not slutty, smart but not brilliant. You are competent at work, but careful not to outshine your coworkers. You work hard and expect to be rewarded and appreciated. If you're single, you play hard-to-get and patiently await Prince Charming's arrival (or proposal), and you regularly survey your deficiencies to make sure you measure up. If you have children, you raise them without complaining or asking for too much help.

Despite the fact that you've followed the good girl rules, something is wrong with your life. You feel vaguely dissatisfied even though you're doing everything you're supposed to do. It's not your fault; what your mother didn't teach you is that although the good girl rules may keep you tidy, seasonably fashionable, reputable, ladylike, pleasant, popular, and silent, they won't make you happy. Consider some of the rules we were taught:

- If you can't say something nice, don't say anything at all.
- Never wear white before Easter or after Labor Day, unless it's winter white.
- Always wear clean underwear in case you get in an accident.
- If you want to land a man, play hard to get.
- A woman's reputation is like fine china. Once it's broken, it can never be repaired.
- A lady should be able to walk on floors without being heard—don't clomp.
- Ladies should sit with their legs together.
- Women are unattractive when they're angry.

How are these good girl rules working for you? If everything's great, then do your unhappy girlfriend a favor and lend her this book. If things are just okay, ask yourself: Am I ready to have more? More money? More power? More passion? More fulfillment? More balance? More respect? More fun? Am I ready to say whatever I want, get angry, sit with my legs wide open, wear white whenever I feel like it, chase men to my heart's content, break fine china, and clomp around in stilettos? If your answers are yes, then get out your stilettos and prepare to take charge of your life.

Psst! We want to let you in on a secret. Being a good girl who follows "the rules" gets you nowhere fast; it keeps you exactly where you are—in your place. It holds you back, keeps you from reaching your potential, and ensures that you are nonthreatening, not earning too much money, not attaining too much power, or not getting too uppity. But is it really a good thing to be bad? you ask yourself. Yes, it is. That's what *Climbing Mountains in Stilettos* is about: the good that comes from being a bad girl and the bad that comes from being a good girl. By writing this book, we hope to inspire bad behavior that will lead to wickedly good results.

So *who* is a bad girl? Most bad girls are just like you and me: they're family members, colleagues or acquaintances—people we look up to because they seem to sail through life, getting everything they ever wished for. And you can be sure that their lives will always be better than yours if you keep following the good girl rules.

More Good Girl Rules

- Why buy the cow when you're getting the milk for free?
- Women aren't complete unless they've had a child.
- Cursing is for tramps and women with potty mouths.
- A good wife makes sure her husband comes home to a hot, delicious meal.
- Sex is a wife's duty.
- You should save yourself for marriage.
- Good girls put family before career.
- Once you have children, your career development is less important than your partner's.
- A wife's income is supplemental to her husband's.
- Girls aren't good at math and science.
- It's not ladylike to talk about menses or menopause.
- If a man takes you out to eat, you should order something dainty and inexpensive.

So *what* is a bad girl exactly? Well, she's not what the movie titles and song lyrics say she is. You know what we're talking about, don't you? "Bad girls" in movies and songs are prostitutes. And we sure aren't going to teach you how to be a prostitute. We'd like to take this phrase and put a positive spin on it. After all, "bad boys" conjures up a positive image for most of us. It doesn't refer to gigolos; it refers to guys who are fun, adventurous, and usually devilishly handsome. Sure, these boys might get into a little trouble, but it's usually not illegal. We all love a bad boy, don't we? But what about a bad girl?

Is a bad girl cruel, catty, and conniving? No, but she's in touch with her inner bitch and can summon her at will. When she does, hold on to your miniskirts! It doesn't even occur to her that giving someone a piece of her mind might offend. And she doesn't tolerate being pushed around—if some people find that offensive, so be it.

Imagine Cat Woman outside the shadow of Batman and Robin—she's a force to contend with, a woman brimming with attitude, style, and grace, poised on four-inch stilettos, and wrapped up in leather. And she's got enough verve and nerve to light up the bat cave ten times over. A bad girl is better than a good man and a whole lot more interesting than a bad boy. No, that description doesn't quite do her justice. Think about her like this: A bad girl is a girl or woman who

- blazes her own trail,
- removes obstacles from her path,
- defends herself against attacks, and
- fights back when threatened.

What *makes* a woman a bad girl? Does she have to be born one or is it something she can learn? Well, a few lucky women were born bad, but most bad girls are good girls who had a wake-up call. After years of the good girl routine, they got pushed too far one too many times, or they just woke up one day and realized their lives were not unfolding the way they'd planned—and it wasn't their fault. They were doing all the right things—getting an education, working hard, being responsible, and helping others—but things just weren't working out. They weren't making enough money, they didn't have satisfying relationships, or they were being taken for granted. Plus, they weren't having any fun. Being good gets old.

It doesn't really matter if you slowly inch your way to bad girlhood or become an overnight bad girl sensation. The important thing is that you become one. Trust us; this is the best conversion experience you'll ever have! We know we've got some work ahead of us. Changing the meaning of things doesn't happen overnight. Positive traits in a man such as "bad boy-ishness" are often seen as negative traits in a woman. Don't believe us? Check this out:

A Table of Double Standards

Man	Woman
Hard work and persistence make him a go-getter.	Hard work and persistence make her too serious.
Sleeping around makes him a player.	Sleeping around makes her a slut.
When he's a really nice guy, everyone says he's got a great career ahead of him.	When she's nice, she's not tough enough to get the job done.
When he's moody, he's having an artistic moment.	When she's moody, she's PMSing.
When he grays at the temples, he looks distinguished.	When she grays at the temples, she looks like an old hag or a witch.
When he's irrational, he's having a bad day.	When she's irrational, she's crazy.
When a man is hard to deal with, it's probably because he has a lot on his plate.	When a woman is hard to deal with, she's a cranky bitch who just needs to get laid.
Staying focused on getting the job done makes him a "no nonsense" kind of guy.	Staying focused on getting the job done makes her suspect. "Who the hell does she think she is anyway? Is she too good for a little small talk?"
When he fights for what he wants, he's got balls. When he spends time with the kids, he's a great dad.	When she fights for what she wants, she's a pushy bitch. When she spends time with the kids, she's just doing what's expected of her.

When he's the driving force behind a hugely successful company, he's a visionary. (Think: Bill Gates.)	When she's the driving force behind a hugely successful company, she's a ruthless monster. (Think: Martha Stewart.)

See any pattern here? It's hard not to. There's a double standard. Some of the very same characteristics that are seen as positive in men are negative in women. Take uppity, assertive, focused, or driven women. They all get lumped into one category. Is our culture so unimaginative, rigid, and backward that any woman who isn't pleasing and accommodating is perceived negatively?

We all know women who are conniving, condescending, or just downright mean. But when they're just trying to get what they want and they're not shy about it, shouldn't we applaud these women? Don't we want to be like them? Aren't some of *us* these women?

Now for the "F" word. Some of you might object and say, hey, you're trying to peddle feminism! Feminism's passé. It's so retro. We don't relate to those women from the sixties and seventies who had no sense of humor and hated men. And we sure aren't going to stop shaving our legs or wearing bras.

Check out the dictionary definition of *feminism:* belief in the full social, economic, and political equality of women and men. Now you're probably thinking, I'm not against that. I think men and women should have equal opportunities, equal pay, and equal rights. That's feminist thinking.

Still, for some of us, feminism conjures up a negative image. Feminists are those raging radicals holding protest signs with hairy armpits and bouncing breasts who do lots of angry shouting. But, if you think about it, what's wrong with being a radical? Don't we need radicals? Do you think change is *easy*? That it just *happens* on its own? Don't you think somebody had to kick up some dust to clear the path for change? Well, feminists in the sixties and seventies did. Thanks to them, creepy men can't get away with coming on to you at work; your boss is just as likely to be a man as a woman; you don't have to risk pregnancy every time you have sex; and date rape is no longer our dirty secret but a crime punishable by law.

Feminists teamed up, strapped on their funky seventies footwear, and blazed new trails, making it possible for us to reach our peak potential with a lot less sweating and cursing. Today's bad girl doesn't have to be a myopic raging radical. She can be simultaneously powerful and sexy, assertive and feminine, and ambitious and nurturing.

But our climbing days are not over. We've come a long way in the last thirty or forty years, but there are still summits we haven't reached, and trails that are only partly cleared for us. Think about it this way: History doesn't reverse itself in a few decades. Luckily, bad girls love a challenge. But climbing mountains is not a solo ascent; we have to team up with other women to get to the next trail marker. So all you bad girls out there, let's strap on our packs, tighten up our shoelaces, drag some good girls with us, and hit the trail.

So, how far are you on the trail? Take the *Bad Girl Quiz* at the end of most chapters and find out if you're on your way to the summit or if you're stuck at the bottom of a crevasse. Read each question carefully and then circle yes, no, or sometimes.

BAD GIRL QUIZ

1. I am comfortable calling myself a bad girl.
   a. Yes b. No c. Sometimes
2. I'm a good girl when the situation calls for it.
   a. Yes b. No c. Sometimes
3. I worry that people think I'm overbearing and rude when I'm being firm or forceful.
   a. Yes b. No c. Sometimes
4. I break rules when it would benefit me.
   a. Yes b. No c. Sometimes
5. If you push me, I'll push back.
   a. Yes b. No c. Sometimes
6. I think outspoken women are unattractive.
   a. Yes b. No c. Sometimes
7. I identify with the feminist way of thinking.
   a. Yes b. No c. Sometimes
8. I will risk confrontation to get what I want.
   a. Yes b. No c. Sometimes
9. I think that motherhood is the most fulfilling role for a woman.
   a. Yes. b. No c. Sometimes
10. I think that ambitious women have unhappy personal lives.
   a. Yes b. No c. Sometimes

11. I think the fight for women's equality has been won.
     a. Yes   b. No

Answers:
1. a. 2 , b. 0, c. 1
2. a. 0, b. 2, c. 1
3. a. 0, b. 2, c. 1
4. a. 2, b. 0, c. 1
5. a. 2, b. 0, c. 1
6. a. 0, b. 2, c. 1

7. a. 2, b. 0, c. 1
8. a. 2, b. 0, c. 1
9. a. 0, b. 1, c. 2
10. a. 0, b. 2, c. 1
11. a. 0, b.2

What was your score and what does it mean? Well, the bigger your score, the badder the bad girl. Find out where you fall on the bad girl scale.

Bad Girl Scale

22 Only!	Stiletto Girl
16–21	Platform Girl
11–15	Wedge Girl
6–10	Cuban Girl
0–5	Kitten Girl

Good Is a Four-Letter Word

Think about this: Why are women so often described with light, airy words like *perky*, *bubbly*, or *good*? Is "good" really good for everyone? Can men be bubbly and perky or are those words reserved for women we don't take very seriously?

When is the last time you heard anyone say about a *man:*

- He slept his way to the top.
- What a bubbly personality he has.
- Perkiness is what makes him our top salesman.
- He's good at sales because he's so attractive.

If you're as tired of these descriptors as we are, what words would you rather hear to describe you? Here are a few we came up with:

- She's brilliant—always one step ahead of everyone.
- She's full of ideas—a real creative genius.
- She's got vision.
- She doesn't take no for an answer.
- She's got nerves of steel.
- She doesn't put up with any grief from anyone.

Breaking the Fine China

Remember the good girl rule: A woman's reputation is like fine china. Once it's broken, it can never be repaired. We're giving you permission to break the fine china—to hold it overhead and smash it into smithereens.

In this activity, you will first identify the good girl rules you've lived by. Then you will come up with a plan to shatter the rule—to break the fine china. (You can use the ones included in this chapter or make up your own.)

Trail Tip: This is very cathartic and freeing. You'll feel light on your feet after all the breakage; you may even sprout wings.

Example:
Rule: I have to learn to cook so I can cook for my husband.
Breaking the Rule: I married a chef.

Example:
Rule 1:
Breaking the Rule:

Rule 2:
Breaking the Rule:

Rule 3:
Breaking the Rule:

WHO NEEDS FEMINISM?

Take this quiz to find out how much you know about the state of the world's women. Is feminism still necessary, or is it obsolete?

1. Out of over 180 countries, how many have elected women to heads of state or government?
   - a. 14
   - b. 37
   - c. 49
   - d. 73
2. What is the leading cause of injury and death for women worldwide?
   - a. car accidents
   - b. domestic violence
   - c. assault
   - d. suicide
3. In the United States a woman is battered by her partner every_____.
   - a. 3 seconds
   - b. 5 seconds
   - c. 9 seconds
   - d. 10 minutes

4. In the United States a woman is raped every_____.

    a. 1 minute

    b. 3 minutes

    c. 20 minutes

    d. 45 minutes

5. In over sixty of the world's states, women's income is ___ lower than men's income.

    a. 10%

    b. 20%

    c. 40%

    d. 50%

6. In the United States women hold 50.3% of all management and professional positions, but what percentage of Fortune 500 CEO positions do they hold?

    a. 1.4%

    b. 8.5%

    c. 20.7%

    d. 35%

7. Approximately 855 million people in the world are illiterate. What percentage is female?

    a. 25%

    b. 50%

    c. 70%

    d. 85%

8. Across the globe, women often work how many more hours per week than men?

a. 15

b. 20

c. 35

d. 40

9. Women produce nearly 80% of the food on the planet, but receive less than _____ of agricultural assistance.

    a. 10%

    b. 20%

    c. 30%

    d. 50%

10. Which country still doesn't have universal suffrage?

    a. Brunei Darussalam

    b. Saudi Arabia

    c. United Arab Emirates

    d. all the above

Answers: 1. a, 2. b, 3. c, 4. b, 5. d, 6. a, 7. c, 8. c, 9. a, 10. d

Pioneer Pass

Remember, Ginger Rogers did everything Fred
Astaire did, but backwards and in high heels.
—Faith Whittlesey

About This Trail: If you find your way to Pioneer
Pass, you'll be a woman who changes the course of
history. If you don't, your destiny is uncertain.

Duration: You'll be on this trail for as long as it takes
you to realize that it wasn't Eve's fault.

Distance: It starts at the Garden of Eden, where Eve
threw the apple at Adam and hooked up with the
snake. It ends on top of the world.

Difficulty: Extremely radical ascent. This one's not for good girls, sissies, or distressed damsels. Only daring divas can reach the end of this trail. It requires bushwhacking, switchbacking, and rock scrambling.

Elevation: This trail summits at a dizzying elevation. If your hair stands on end, don't become a lightning rod.

Backpack Essentials: An apple, navigation tools, and revisionist history.

What to Leave Behind: Betsy Ross, bonnets, fainting couches, corsets, crumpets, the history of good girls, and the history of men at war.

Early Pitfalls: Vertigo, altitude sickness, and getting lost. A bushwhacker who gets lost becomes a search and rescue victim.

Trail Tip: Bushwhack with confidence, keeping in mind what women are capable of. You must have the ability to lose yourself in your adventure without ever losing touch with where you are.

At the Trail's End: On Pioneer Pass you'll discover that the bad girls of history have talked back, spoken out, pushed limits, acted with grit, risked it all, and succeeded by being themselves. This trail will help you understand where you've come from to know where you're going.

Some history books would have us believe that women throughout the ages were only donning bonnets, sewing flags, mending fences, serving tea, and delicately puttering about baking biscuits in homes on the range.

After you've climbed Pioneer Pass, you will realize that nothing could be further from the truth. Bad girls have changed the course of history: skippered pirate ships, piloted solo flights, pioneered painting styles, outwitted male colleagues, and hung on crosses for their beliefs.

Now, you may be thinking, what do these girls of history have to do with me? These pioneering women are your guides on this trail. They showed the world that a woman's place is not just in the home; it is also at sea, in the sky, in front of an easel, at the *New Yorker,* and wherever she pleases on a bus.

These women didn't play by the rules; didn't doubt their abilities; didn't take no for an answer; and didn't let their lives be shaped by other people's limited imaginations. They lived their lives to the fullest and all of us are better off because of them.

The girls in this history lesson include women who made the climb up to the bad girl summit so that the rest of us could enjoy the view from the top. We chose stories of women who trailblazed, hell-raised, dream-gazed, and simply amazed.

While men have been parading around in stiff uniforms with unfortunate hats, killing each other at war, women have been busy building and creating culture and communities.

We'll start with a pirate queen from sixteenth-century Ireland and end with a sassy performer.

The Pirate

Grainne (Gran-ya) O'Malley was a pirate queen from Galway, Ireland, born in 1530. Grainne was a notorious pirate, seafarer, trader, and chieftain. She was once condemned to death, but later granted a pardon after she charmed the socks (or the corset) off Queen Elizabeth I.

Grainne's father was the chieftain of a clan of renowned mariners, traders, and pirates. As a child, she dreamed of joining him at sea, but her mother resisted, claiming the life of a sailor was not proper for young ladies. When Grainne pleaded with her father to accompany him on a trading expedition, he refused, saying that her long hair would get tangled in the ship's ropes. Being the cunning girl that she was, she chopped off her hair in protest. It was then that her family gave her the nickname Grainne Mhaol (Grace the Bald). She was permitted to join her father on the first of many expeditions she would take in her lifetime.

Grace became an intrepid leader by land and sea—a chief of a private army, and a captain of a fleet of ships that she sailed along the Atlantic coastline south to Portugal and north into the Baltic. She imported wine, port, silks, and amber to Ireland. Grace and her shipmates dabbled in piracy; a common strategy was to intercept a merchant ship and demand payment for its safe passage.

Grace didn't let social customs constrain her. She retaliated for the murders of her husband and lover, divorced her second husband, and gave birth aboard her ship. Legend has it that that Grace's son was born on the high seas while Grace was returning from a trading voyage. Her son was just one day old when Grace's ship was attacked by Turkish pirates. When Grace's captain warned her that pirates were about to overtake the ship, she strapped on her weapons and stormed into battle. It is said that the sight of a wild woman terrified the Turks, who were then easily defeated. Talk about juggling work and family!

Grace was a true pioneer—a woman as empowered as any in our modern era. Four centuries after commanding at sea, she continues to challenge our preconceived notions and societal expectations of women's roles. We may be able to envision female pirates in a Hollywood film, but a real female pirate is considered the stuff of legends and tall tales. Grace succeeded as a seafarer, trader, and pirate while still maintaining her femininity—the hallmarks of a true bad girl.

The Pilot

> The woman who can create her own job is the woman who will win fame and fortune.
> —Amelia Earhart

Amelia Earhart was a woman of many firsts. She was the first woman to fly across the Atlantic, in 1928, and the first person to fly solo from Hawaii to California, in 1935. She disappeared attempting to become the first woman to fly around the world.

As a girl, she was a daredevil sledder, an avid tree climber, and a rat hunter. She collected articles about prominent women in male-dominated fields. No doubt she drew inspiration from learning about women who were breaking the mold of femininity.

Amelia discovered her passion for flying when she attended a stunt-flying exhibition at the age of twenty. In 1920, pilot Frank Hawks took her for a life-changing ride in his plane. Amelia declared, "By the time I had gotten two or three hundred feet off the ground, I knew I had to fly."

During World War I, Amelia worked as a nurse's aide in a military hospital; she also attended college, and later became a social worker. She took her first flying lesson in January of 1921 and by June she had saved enough money to buy herself a plane. The plane was a bright yellow two-seater biplane. Amelia flew this plane, named *Canary,* when she set her first women's record by flying at an altitude of 14,000 feet.

One afternoon in April of 1928, Amelia received at work what she thought was a prank call. The caller asked her if she would like to fly the Atlantic. Once she realized the caller was for real, she said yes without a moment's hesitation.

Amelia had been invited to join pilot Wilmer Bill Stultz and copilot Louis Gordon. On June 17, the team flew from Newfoundland to Wales in approximately twenty-one hours. Their landmark flight received worldwide attention, and the crew was given a welcome home reception with a ticker-tape parade in New York. The team was also honored by President Calvin Coolidge at the White House.

While preparing for the flight across the Atlantic, Amelia developed an interest in George Putnam, her publicist. The two first became friends, and were later married. Determined to retain her independence after they wedded, she referred to their marriage as a "partnership" with "dual control." With Putnam she flew in tandem, but with the ability to fly solo at any time.

Amelia Earhart is known for her courage, vision, and groundbreaking accomplishments, both in aviation and for women. Her words, written in a letter to her husband in the event that she died while flying, capture the essence of her spirit. She wrote, "Please know I am quite aware of the hazards. I want to do it because I want to do it. Women must try to do things as men have tried. When they fail, their failure must be but a challenge to others."

Perhaps her disappearance, an unfinished story, has challenged other women to start where Amelia left off.

The Painter

I live life in the margins of society,
and the rules of normal society don't apply to
those who live on the fringe.
—Tamara de Lempicka

Tamara de Lempicka (1898–1980) is one of the most famous painters of the art deco period. She braved the Russian Revolution, fled to Paris, and captured the Roaring Twenties on canvas.

Tamara was born in Poland and moved to Russia, where she lived until the Bolsheviks arrested her husband during the Russian Revolution. She escaped the revolution, and later sneaked her husband out of the country by offering sexual favors to a government official in exchange for her husband's release. The couple escaped to Paris.

Once in France, Tamara was determined to earn a living from painting. She tirelessly studied the techniques and styles of Michelangelo and Botticelli and began painting in her signature style—grand, chunky, and erotic nudes. Her works were cubist with the sensuality of the Italian Renaissance painters. She became a well-known art deco portrait painter.

Tamara's paintings were well received in the 1925 art deco exhibition in Paris and in solo exhibitions. Despite her success, she was not as renowned as some of her male contemporaries. At that time, it was difficult for female painters to achieve commercial success unless they were linked to a prominent male artist.

Her life as an artist was only part of the picture; her social life was scandalous and raucous, especially for a woman of her time. Tamara slept with actresses, prostitutes, diplomats, and sailors. She guzzled gin fizzes with upper-crust Parisians and hosted wild parties with naked girls posing as human caviar dishes. During her lesbian phase, she arranged decadent delights on her girlfriends' bodies and indulged in midnight snacks.

Her biographer, Laura Claridge, proclaims that Tamara has been denied her deserved place in modern art history because she was a woman before her time. Claridge even proposes that the history of modernism be rewritten so that Tamara's brilliance is no longer overlooked.

Sadly, this is true of many great women who have been overshadowed by their male contemporaries. Undoubtedly, much of the history of arts and letters should be rewritten to bring brilliant women out of the shadows and into the limelight where they belong.

The Poet

> That woman speaks eighteen languages
> and can't say no in any of them.
> —Dorothy Parker

Dorothy Parker (1893–1967), an American short story writer, poet, and screenwriter, was best known for her acerbic wit and sarcasm, especially related to taboo subjects, such as suicide.

Dorothy was a bad girl from the very start. While a student at the Blessed Sacrament Convent School in New York City, she earned a reputation among the nuns as a troublemaker. They expelled her for claiming that the Immaculate Conception was a form of "spontaneous combustion."

Unlike many women of her time, she ventured out on her own after high school graduation, supporting herself by working in a bookstore and playing the piano at night. This gave her time to write poetry during the day. In 1913 she became a drama critic at *Vanity Fair* and married her first husband, Edwin Pond Parker. Two years later, she published her first verse in *Vogue* magazine, who hired her as a caption writer.

A bad girl of the 1900s, Dorothy's verbal wit and satire got her in trouble. She was fired from *Vanity Fair* for, according to her, "having opinions at a magazine that had no opinions."

Being opinionated can indeed be a liability, but Dorothy demonstrated that setbacks don't keep a bad girl down for long. She went on to become the only female member of the Algonquin Round Table, an elite intellectual and literary circle that included the founder of the *New Yorker*. In 1925, Dorothy was hired to write book reviews for the magazine. Dorothy began to publish volumes of poetry. Her first collection of poems, *Enough Rope*, was published in 1926. This collection became a bestseller. Other volumes of poetry include *Sunset Gun* (1928), *Death and Taxes* (1931), and *Not So Deep as a Well* (1936). In the 1930s, Dorothy published three collections of short stories: *Lament for the Living* (1930), *After Such Pleasures* (1933), and *Here Lies* (1939).

Also in the 1930s, Dorothy moved to Hollywood with her second husband and turned her attention to screenwriting, working on a number of films including *A Star Is Born* and *Queen for a Day*. She became a Hollywood hotshot, earning up to $2,500 a week, a generous salary during the Great Depression. Dorothy and two other writers founded the Screenwriters Guild, her lasting contribution to the film industry.

She joined the Communist Party, and protested Fascism through her tireless support of the Republican side during the Spanish Civil War. Dorothy made dangerous liaisons that eventually resulted in blacklisting and troubles with the House Un-American Activities Committee during the McCarthy period.

Upon her death, Dorothy left her estate to civil rights leader Martin Luther King, Jr.

The Protester

The only tired I was, was tired of giving in.
—Rosa Parks

Whoever said that one person can't change the world hasn't heard the story of Rosa Parks.

Rosa is famous for her refusal to obey a bus driver's order that she relinquish her seat to a white man. By refusing to give up her seat, Parks challenged the South's Jim Crow laws and Montgomery's segregated bus seating policy that were at play in the 1950s.

She is known as the mother of the civil rights movement. Her act of civil disobedience and her subsequent arrest and trial set off a chain of historic events. These included the Montgomery Bus Boycott, one of the largest and most effective mass movements against racial segregation in history. It also propelled Martin Luther King, Jr., an organizer of the boycott, to the forefront of the civil rights movement.

Most people are familiar with the story of the African American woman who wouldn't give up her seat on the bus. The story that is not well known is her life prior to her arrest. Refusing to cooperate with the bus driver on that fateful day was not the first action she took to correct injustice. Parks served as secretary of the National Association for the Advancement of Colored People (NAACP) and adviser to the NAACP Youth Council. She tried to register to vote several times, but the voter registration process made it nearly impossible for blacks to successfully register. Before the watershed bus incident, Parks had a number of clashes with bus drivers. In discussing the humiliation, she said, "I didn't want to pay my fare and then go around the back door, because many times, even if you did that, you might not get on the bus at all. They'd probably shut the door, drive off, and leave you standing there."

Rosa wasn't a sassy, outspoken bad girl; rather she was a reserved woman of inner fortitude who was tired of tolerating mistreatment. In her 1995 book *Quiet Strength* she wrote, "All I felt was tired. Tired of being pushed around. Tired of seeing the bad treatment and disrespect of children, women, and men just because of the color of their skin."

The next time you find yourself thinking that you would like to initiate change, but you don't feel that you alone can make a difference, remember Rosa Parks—one woman who changed the nation forever with an act of silent protest.

The Performer

I'm not going to die because I failed as someone else. I'm going to succeed as myself.
—Margaret Cho

Imagine that you were asked to star in a TV show, but you were told that you were too fat to play yourself. Margaret Cho, a very successful stand-up comedian, was told by the producers of her prime-time sitcom *All-American Girl* that she would have to lose weight to play herself. Bear in mind that her trade was comedy, not fashion modeling. What did her weight have to do with her ability to make people laugh? Trying to play by the rules of show biz, where a size eight is considered unfortunate, she began to practice various methods of starvation and lost a significant amount of weight in a short period. In her film *I'm the One That I Want,* she recounts being so hungry all the time that she could hardly focus on her lines. Her weight loss was so extreme that she landed in the hospital with kidney failure and nearly died—starvation in exchange for a moment of fame. In the end, the show was canceled and Margaret was devastated.

Playing by the rules of Hollywood, Margaret lost weight, her outrageously funny voice, her sassy spirit, and nearly her life. But she didn't stay down for long. She bounced back with a vengeance and an irreverent attitude; she decided that her gift for comedy was not going to be controlled by any bottom-gazing producers in Hollywood boardrooms. In Margaret's case, being good was as good as being dead. Now she's relishing her wickedly funny ways and loving every minute of it! So, incidentally, are her audiences.

Tracing the Tracks on Pioneer Pass

What do all these bad girls of history have in common? They didn't hesitate to speak their minds; they pursued their dreams and let passion drive their lives; they weren't afraid of offending; they took actions to change injustice; and they used their platforms to make their marks on the world. These bad girls are colorful, passionate, inspiring, outrageous, and courageous.

The bottom line—they weren't afraid. Or if they were, they didn't let fear stop them. Let their lives be an inspiration to you. Like these bad girls, you can sail, fly, paint, write, entertain, and change the world through your unique expression. What are you waiting for?

Before you head out to make your mark, take some time to compose a quote for yourself—a motto for the life you want to live. Who says that famous women are the only ones worth quoting?

Quotable You

Imagine you are in your final days on earth, looking back on the life you created for yourself. What were the words that you lived by?

Example:

"Dance like no one is watching, love like you've never been hurt, sing like no one is listening, and live like it's heaven on earth."

—Anonymous

Your Quote:

_____

_____

Scaring Yourself

Reading about these bad girls of history from the comfort of your sofa or Lazy Girl is only part of completing Pioneer Pass. The other part is following their lead and doing something every day that scares you—not something self-destructive, like driving as if you're on the autobahn on a foggy night or skydiving without a parachute, but something that takes you out of your comfort zone. It may be difficult at first, but you'll soon realize how exhilarating and freeing it is to scare yourself. You may even scare fear right out of your life! We'd love to hear from you about how scaring yourself is going. We'll feature your scared stories on our website.

Take some time to think about the things you're most afraid of. Then come up with a plan to scare yourself out of hiding.

1. What I'm afraid of:
   What I'll do to scare myself:
2. What I'm afraid of:
   What I'll do to scare myself:
3. What I'm afraid of:
   What I'll do to scare myself:

Sleeping Mountain Lion Pass

A lion among ladies is a most dreadful thing.
—William Shakespeare

About This Trail: You're in mountain lion territory, which is ideal for bad girls. It's rough, dangerous, and oh-so-adventurous. It's also chock-full of wild animals, so remember the golden rule: Don't feed them. Mountain lions and bad girls can fend for themselves.

Duration: As long as it takes for the bad girl to awaken from her slumber. Sleeping Beauty slept for one hundred years, and what did it get her? Don't make that mistake! Once the bad girl wakes up and straps on a sturdy pair of hiking boots, it's a fast climb to the top.

Distance: If you think you don't need this one, you've got a long way to go!

Difficulty: The good girl will cry "I don't wanna go" the whole way up. But once she gets to the top and sees the view, she won't want to come down.

Elevation: A mountain pass is the highest point on a trail through a mountain range, so it's pretty high. Think vertigo, nausea, or complete and utter disorientation if you just awoke from a good girl catnap.

Backpack Essentials: Strap on the stiletto heel lifts (inserts for your hiking boots) and inhale an energy bar; bells to alert the sleeping lion.

What to Leave Behind: Those darn glass slippers. How many times do we have to tell you that climbing mountains in stilettos (or glass slippers for that matter) is a metaphor, not a fashion tip?

Early Pitfalls: You miss the trailhead. This trail is invisible to good girls. From their perspective (clearly seen from a crevasse instead of a summit), they have already climbed every mountain and forded every stream (do we hear Julie Andrews in the nunnery)? They don't need to climb up a mountain pass—or so they think. Bad girls, you'll have to drag good girls kicking and screaming up this one.

Trail Tip: Make some noise. Remember, the goal is to wake the sleeping mountain lion, that is, the bad girl.

At the Trail's End: Getting on this trail implies a commitment from you: you're ready to stir the hibernating bad girl and leave the good girl behind—forever. It takes a leap of faith to leave the familiar behind and enter uncharted territory. But you should know that the good girl path will not take you to the places you really want to go.

———————————

For most of us, right around the time we begin to make the transition from wobbly cub to full-grown lioness, the good girl takes over and the bad girl goes into hibernation. Sometimes she wakes up later in life. Sometimes she doesn't. The good girl has lowered expectations and fewer delusions of grandeur, has forgotten that she's strong and courageous, and has developed a serious case of body image obsession.

Carol's bad girl went into hiding when she was just a tween. Previously, she had been one of the fastest, cockiest, smartest girls at her school. She tied for the fastest time in the obstacle course (for girls or boys). She got straight A's in all her classes except math, a subject that was rejected early on by her nonlinear, imaginative mind. She loved to compete in school and sports, and she regularly rumbled with bullies on the playground. But then her body started changing, and so did everyone's expectations of her. She crumbled under the pressure to be this new, perfect object that people were reflecting back at her. She became a borderline anorexic, skipping lunch and sometimes dinner, doing extra exercises after a full day of school, practice, chores, and homework. She became withdrawn, reserved, and suppressed her dreams of being an artist and adventurer. Her bad girl, however, did not last long in captivity. How did she escape? Well, she was needed. After changing schools a few times and having her heart broken, she couldn't withstand the biggest loss of all: her old self. By age twenty she'd reclaimed her dreams to entertain, which took the form of modern dance and writing, to have adventures (first stop: war-torn Central America), and to live an artist's life with her now longtime love, a musician.

Ann's friend, Cathy, went into hiding at the age of twelve. As a girl, she was a rough and tumble tomboy with four brothers. Cathy was tough, spunky, full of life, and confident. Then, when she hit adolescence, the tomboy disappeared. Cathy swapped tree climbing for calorie counting, kickball playing for Tab drinking, and mischievous pranks for boy pleasing. What emerged was a weight-obsessed, depressed, despondent, helpless teenage girl. Where did the tomboy go? Why did she slip into hiding?

Twenty years later, her adventurous spirit reemerged when she became an avid rock climber—tackling climbs such as El Capitan in Yosemite, a steep rock wall that takes a week to ascend. The calorie-counting business is a thing of the past; she's now counting the number of climbing ascents she has made.

So what were you like before the good girl took over? Try to remember how you felt about yourself when you were eight, nine, and ten years old. We've talked to many women who say they felt more self-possessed at this age than anytime since. Maybe you were cocky, tomboyish, feisty, silly, smart-as-a-whip, and bursting with dreams and ambitions. You were going to be the star of your own variety show, just like Cher, and a gold medalist at both the summer and the winter Olympics. (Okay, maybe those were Carol's dreams, not yours.)

The point is you may now be a sleeping bad girl. What happens to girls who nod off just as their lives are starting to develop? Nothing good. Think of Dorothy in the *Wizard of Oz*. At first, she's fearful and passive, but she didn't let go of her dream to get back home. How did she finally get her wish? She found her courage. She confronted the all-powerful Oz and melted the wicked witch. Being a good girl, ruby slippers and all, got her nowhere in her journey.

The Sleeping Bad Girl

A mountain lion is nocturnal, secretive, and rarely seen, but that doesn't mean she doesn't exist. The same is true for the sleeping bad girl. Like a mountain lion, she is elusive, but she's poised to pounce as soon as the right opportunity comes her way.

Okay, so let's say you decide you don't want to awaken the bad girl for one reason or another. You've decided that you like your good girl life just the way it is, and summoning the bad girl is too much trouble, too dangerous, too risky, or too scary. A sleeping cat should never be disturbed, right? Wrong. A trapped animal will wage destruction on her surroundings when released. Ann's mother could tell you that.

Ann's mother told her a story about breaking up her marriage that was the inspiration for this chapter.

She called Ann one day and said, "You know—I tried for the first thirty-five years of my life to be good, to do everything I was supposed to, but I was miserable. The only power I had was to complain. I owe your poor father an apology. I had no awareness of my shadow side. So, when this charming, handsome manipulator came into my life and appealed to the hidden part of me, I took the bait."

If Ann's mother had been less constricted by the stranglehold of the good girl, she might not have been under the spell of the submerged bad girl. She was desperate to get out, imprisoned; she worked in destructive ways. She continued, "I wreaked havoc on my life—I left your father after twelve years, my four children, and a very comfortable life. What was I thinking? I guess the point is, I wasn't. I traded my life for an unstable marriage to a man of questionable character. I woke up two years later and realized what I had done. It was like waking up in a war-torn area only I was the one who dropped the bomb."

The Awakening

The crouching bad girl climbs out of her hiding place and surveys her surroundings. When she does, you may feel a gnawing sense of dissatisfaction with your life, but you won't quite understand your growing discontent. The return of the bad girl can be brought on by a major life change or a series of events: a parents' divorce, a tough breakup, the birth of a child, a layoff, or yet another disappointing experience with a partner, friend, or colleague. Or it may arrive after many years of being good and getting nowhere and watching others race ahead by doing things good girls were told not to do.

The awakening may be slow and gradual.
For some, it begins as a gentle purr that emerges in the quiet spaces of their lives. The bad girl, long since forgotten, is tired of the solitary confinement. "Why can't I come out and play? Aren't I the more fun, passionate, courageous one?" she asks. "And why was I tucked away in this godforsaken place anyway?" she demands to know.

The good girl feels threatened, and readies herself for a fight. "I am not letting her back into this house. She'll tear things up; she'll pee all over the carpet. Scoot, bad girl, scoot," scolds the good girl. But the bad girl wants back into your life, so she makes progress. Slowly but gradually, a new woman emerges . . .

The awakening may be fast and furious.
You may begin to sabotage yourself and your relationships—like there's a force at play that is out of your control. You rebel against forces in your life that

are holding you back: your job, your partner, your children, or your attitude. Depression, anger, fury, anxiety, and dissatisfaction may all be signs that the bad girl has stirred and is coming out of her lair! A sense of urgency takes you by surprise, grabs hold of your life. You pounce. You quit your thankless job; sell your house and move to Italy; have a passionate love affair; buy a one-way ticket to paradise without the husband or kids; take to the stage; publish a book of poetry; come out of the closet; go on a month-long Buddhist retreat; write a book about bad girls; toss your old wardrobe; shave your head; pierce and tattoo various body parts; and live greedily on the adrenaline created by the constant change.

The Moral of the Tale

How does this story end? Must good triumph over evil? In this case, bad *must* triumph over good. That is, the bad girl must win. If she doesn't, no girl is safe. The world isn't safe. Not convinced of the dangers of staying a good girl? Consider this. The dangers of good girlhood are not unlike the ones you'll encounter if you go off into the wilderness without enough food, water, layers of clothes, or a compass.

1. **You'll be eaten alive—or someone will have you for dinner.**

Growing weak from a lack of sustenance, you become easy prey. Wild animals hunt and kill the weak, and humans are no different. A good girl is a weak girl and her days are numbered. Still think letting the bad girl out is too risky?

2. **You'll freeze to death.**

You try to take cover during a violent electric storm, but the drop in temperature has chilled you to the bone. You try in vain to generate some body heat, but you can't find your inner flame. A good girl's passions smolder rather than burn. So what are your options? Play with fire or let the bad girl out.

3. **You'll get lost—forever.**

But what is the biggest danger of staying a good girl? Getting lost—forever. The good girl hasn't fallen off the path; she can't find it. Essentially, she's lost, and no amount of crumbs will lead her to the trail. Every girl has to find her own way through life. And when she doesn't, she loses sight of who she is and what she truly desires. Don't let this happen to you.

Ready to become a bad girl? Then join us on the next trail to the summit, the Yellow Brick Road.

Danger Ahead: The Good Girl

How do you know if you're a good girl? Here are some of the danger signs. If some apply to you, never fear, your bad girl is near.

She doesn't pull her own weight.

Good girls suffer from dependency syndrome. They may declare their independence, but this Little Miss Independence wants other people to make things happen. Telltale signs that a girl has some extra baggage: she's heavily in debt, she doesn't have a career, she's searching for a rescuer, and her vision of the future is having babies on someone else's dime.

She has a victim mentality.

To the good girl, the world is anything but her oyster—even though she sees herself as a precious pearl. Everyone else is to blame for her failings and shortcomings. She is not resilient; minor setbacks spiral into years of aimless drifting. The good girl often requires rescues or interventions from loved ones. For example, after spending tens of thousands of dollars at Victoria's Secret and being on the verge of bankruptcy, the good girl may call a friend and say, "I'm being evicted from my apartment and have nowhere to go. Can I stay with you for a while?"

She has meltdowns.

Good girls are demure, not direct. So when they feel unappreciated, overloaded, helpless, victimized, or just completely exhausted, they don't speak up; they fall apart. And when this happens, good girls want someone to move in for the rescue. What can be done about this? There's nothing anyone can do except hope it never happens again. But it will . . .

She's always on a diet.

A good girl doesn't know how to love her body (or focus on more important things). She tries out every fad diet and makes others feel guilty if they don't go on it with her. The good girl goes on a juice fast for three weeks to secure her man. Don't want to risk heart failure? Lose the good girl routine.

She drags her friends and lovers to mind-numbing functions.

Good girls can't say no. So it means they drag their friends and lovers to all the tedious and annoying affairs they get guilted into: kids' birthday parties with reptiles and clowns, sleepovers for the tweens, Sunday afternoons with the in-laws, church potlucks and bazaars, a friend's fiftieth birthday celebration with karaoke.

She brings out the mediocre in her partner.

Remember when love was all about finding your better half, becoming a better person, finding someone who brings out your best qualities? A good girl doesn't do any of those things. She aims to please, not participate in her partner's growth. She has absolutely no challenges up her sleeve. Those who hook up with a good girl will remain works-(not)-in-progress. Don't like what you see in the mirror? Become a bad girl.

She leaves orgasms up to her partners.

She lets her lover do all the heavy lifting while giving him absolutely no operating instructions. And she's too clean to get down and dirty—even when heavily intoxicated. The good girl is all about composure, control, and good manners. She's too uptight (or is it upright?) to go down on someone or get herself off. Good girl, shmood girl. When it comes to orgasms, bad girls are in the driver's seat.

She fakes it.

She screams with pleasure before she's even been touched. And she writhes and squirms, while simultaneously calling out her lover's name before the party's even gotten started. Hey, guess what? She's faking it. Does this really matter? If you prefer being a live woman as opposed to a blow-up doll, consider wrapping up the good girl and sending her back.

She's a housekeeping dictator.

Cleanliness is next to goodliness for good girls. They equate bad housekeeping with being a bad woman. An unmade bed is a mockery of her good housekeeping standards, not a sign that all is well in the bedroom. Tired of the endless mopping, dusting, and tidying up? Maybe it's time to try getting dirty!

She resents boys' night out.

The good girl disapproves of boys' night out or any social activity that doesn't include her. She's insecure about her place in her partner's life and she'll never let her guy forget it! If a guy is thinking of playing a game of pickup or poker, he should think again. The good girl will cry foul and she'll demand that these activities be cut short. If a guy is tired of playing beat the clock, he should tell her to beat it.

She tries to "fix" her men.

Good girls view all men as potential fixer-uppers. They're a project, a blob of clay that needs forming, a life waiting for a purpose. While a man sees his life as full of risk taking, adventure, and possibility, the good girl sees it as directionless and irresponsible.

She's no fun!

Need we say more? So, what's the alternative? The bad girl. She's a woman who grabs life by the balls (her man's included) and doesn't take no for an answer. She knows how to get what she wants out of life and she's not ashamed to say so.

BAD GIRL QUIZ

1. I clean up after my partner and then complain about it.

    a. Yes   b. No   c. Sometimes

2. I'm underpaid and hesitate to ask for a raise.

    a. Yes   b. No   c. Sometimes

3. I am on a diet—or at least I say I am.

    a. Yes   b. No   c. Sometimes

4. I climax every time I have sex, thanks to either me or my partner.

    a. Yes   b. No   c. Sometimes

5. I expect my partner to make more money than me.

    a. Yes   b. No   c. Sometimes

6. I critique other women's body parts.

    a. Yes   b. No   c. Sometimes

7. I feel foolish calling myself a bad girl.

    a. Yes   b. No   c. Sometimes

8. When I get overwhelmed, I immediately call for help.

    a. Yes   b. No   c. Sometimes

9. I make choices that support the future I'm dreaming about.

    a. Yes   b. No   c. Sometimes

10. When I'm in the mood, I let my partner know.

    a. Yes   b. No   c. Sometimes

Answers:

1. a. 0, b. 2, c. 1   6. a. 0, b. 2, c. 1
2. a. 0, b. 2, c. 1   7. a. 0, b. 2, c. 1
3. a. 0, b. 2, c. 1   8. a. 2, b. 0, c. 1
4. a. 2, b. 0, c. 1   9. a. 2, b. 0, c. 1
5. a. 0, b. 2, c. 1   10. a. 2, b. 0, c. 1

What was your score and what does it mean? Well, the bigger your score, the badder the bad girl. Find out where you fall in the bad girl scale.

Bad Girl Scale

20 Only!   Stiletto Girl
15–19   Platform Girl
10–14   Wedge Girl
5–9   Cuban Girl
0–4   Kitten Girl

Yellow Brick Road

I used to be Snow White, but I drifted.
—Mae West

About This Trail: You're not in Kansas anymore. Dorothy navigated through a land of broomstick-riding witches, munchkins, flying monkeys, and talking scarecrows to reach the Emerald City and transform her life. Her drive to reach this far-flung, verdant city was to seek help to get back home. Follow the Yellow Brick Road and find your way back home to your dazzling bad girl self.

Duration: It's up to you. The Yellow Brick Road stretches from Munchkin land all the way to the Emerald City and Dorothy walked it in less than a day. How long will it take you to let go of the myths that keep you in a strange, inhospitable land?

Distance: This trail takes only three steps: First, you slay the Wicked Witch of Good Girlhood. Second, you steal her stilettos; and then you click your stiletto heels three times and go home!

Difficulty: While Dorothy started out as a damsel in distress, she rapidly learned to form alliances with individuals who wished to help and protect her. Find your allies, and you'll easily skip ahead.

Backpack Essentials: Choose footwear that will empower you, friends who will accompany you, and an attitude that'll keep all things wicked at bay.

What to Leave Behind: A distorted view of reality. Remember that the Wizard of Oz was just a cowardly man and that the Emerald City's lush green hue was created by special glasses. See through the illusion of good girl myths. Only then will "the dreams that you dare to dream" come true.

Early Pitfalls: Fields of sleep-inducing poppies and other seductive distractions that take your focus away from your end goal.

Trail Tip: By helping others on this journey, you'll also help yourself. Join forces with women who need your encouragement, have lost their heart, or who doubt their abilities, and follow the Yellow Brick Road together.

At the Trail's End: Living by myths will turn your life into a fairy tale. On this trail you'll learn that by dispelling myths you can live *your* life instead of Snow White's or Sleeping Beauty's. It will enable you to wake up without a kiss from a prince.

Think about all the pale, depressed maidens who fainted, waited to be kissed by a prince, sought rescue from a castle window, or were fitted for a missing glass slipper. What exactly were these ladies-in-waiting waiting for? Were they so fragile and incompetent that they couldn't get on with life until a man in tights appeared?

What is responsible for the good girl takeover? How is it that a girl can go from a powerful, playful, self-confident person to a shadow of her former self—from a tomboy to a lady-in-waiting? Perhaps it is all the myths, assumptions, and stereotypes that operate in our society and seep into our subconscious, despite our attempts to overcome them.

Although bad girls are influenced by the same assumptions, rules, and myths as good girls, bad girls question and challenge them. Where do you stumble and fall, and how do you regain your footing?

Love

Freefall #1: You're going to meet Prince Charming, fall in love, and live happily ever after.

Catch Yourself: We all know that this probably won't happen, but deep down this is what we expect and hope for. And if it doesn't happen, we believe something is wrong with us—that we're defective somehow. Prince Charming is fine if you want to be locked up in a tower of faulty expectations. Prince Charming, if he ever did exist, was probably overbearing, controlling, and unenlightened. But this is the twenty-first century. We don't live in castles. And princes and princesses get divorced. Consider Lady Di. Her fairy-tale wedding to a prince turned into a troubled marriage, a disturbed life, and a tragic ending.

Regain Your Footing: Look for someone who is real.

Freefall #2: You should wait patiently for a marriage proposal from your boyfriend. Someday it will come…

Catch Yourself: If your relationship is stalled in the slow lane, move it into the fast lane by letting your boyfriend know where you stand. Propose to him or give him an ultimatum. If he wants to be with you, he will step up to the plate. Some men have to be catapulted into manhood by their girlfriends. They'll thank you later. They may be freaked out at first, but they'll get used to their new role. In other words, they'll get over it. If they can't get over it, it means there's no future there.

Regain Your Footing: If your partner loves you, he will take action. If not, the sooner you know he's not in it for the long run, the better.

Freefall #3: If you play hard to get, you'll get the man.

Catch Yourself: Let's put this age-old myth to rest. The truth is, you might not get the man even if you play hard to get. Keeping a man at arm's length when you'd rather be in his arms is totally unfulfilling. You waste time, lose spontaneity, and wind up a lady-in-waiting. Plus, you give all your power to the guy. Eventually, you'll grow to resent this. If there's something between you and him, it doesn't matter who pursues whom. Men who claim that they need the chase will probably move on once they catch you anyway. If they say it's that way in the animal kingdom, tell them to get lost in the jungle!

Regain Your Footing: If you're interested in a man, the sooner you let him know, the better. That way, you can quickly figure out if there's any potential for a relationship, and, if not, you can move on.

Freefall #4: You have to be perfect to find a mate.

Catch Yourself: Actually, you can be striking it rich or living on unemployment, on the way up or on the way down, lucky in love or down on your luck, in shape or out of shape, totally together or coming unhinged, lost or found, on or off your spiritual path, on or off Prozac, on or off your rocker, or on or off the wagon and *still* find a mate. Ann has a friend who was completely broke and struggling with depression when she met her future husband. So far, they're living happily ever after.

Regain Your Footing: Do yourself a favor and drop the perfectionism trip. It is a thankless and lonely journey. You can find a mate in any state.

Freefall #5: You have to have a man to be complete.

Catch Yourself: First of all, lesbians and some intentionally single women do just fine without a man. So let's just rethink this whole "complete" business. Rather than looking outside for your better half, look inward. If you feel as if you are incomplete or missing something, you will most likely find it within yourself.

When you do look for a partner, search for someone who enhances or inspires you—not someone to complete you. In fact, if you believe you are incomplete and look for the missing puzzle piece, you will likely drive away potential partners. They will detect your frantic search mission and be turned off by your desperate attempts to make yourself whole.

Regain Your Footing: If you look for someone to make you whole, you'll probably attract a "project" or a fixer-upper. When it comes to intimate relationships, two halves don't make a whole.

Freefall #6: You can't make it without a man.

Catch Yourself: You wanna bet? Look around and you'll see plenty of women thriving professionally, financially, personally, emotionally, and spiritually without a man. In fact, it's better to be alone than to be with a man who drains and depletes you. If your partner isn't helping make you the best you can be, he isn't the right choice.

Regain Your Footing: You can find the match to your own glass slipper.

Sex

Freefall #1: You shouldn't be promiscuous.

Catch Yourself: Actually, exploring your sexuality in a safe and healthy way is a good thing. You can discover what works best for you and be ready to ask for that in any sexual encounter. If you take control of your sexuality, it won't take control of you. And it could help you avoid relationship landmines. In the end, you will probably make wiser relationship choices if your libido is not in charge. Ann has a friend who just ended a bad ten-year marriage who said this about her husband: "He was gorgeous and I should have screwed his brains out three times. Instead, I married him and paid for my bad decision for over a decade."

Regain Your Footing: Women need one-night stands too. (But remember, wrap him up in latex to keep away those infectious STDs!)

Freefall #2: Women have more trouble getting off than men do.

Catch Yourself: While the orgasmic success rate for women may be lower than for men, most men over eighteen are not the sexual machines they claim to be. There are plenty of low performers who can't get aroused when they're tired or stressed or when they're feeling blue. There are even a few who can't get turned on at all because they think that sex is dirty. Worse yet, we know of men who let their emotions get in the way . . . sound familiar?

Regain Your Footing: Your libido ebbs and flows and so does your partner's.

Freefall #3: A woman's sexual behavior places her in one of two categories: virgin or whore.

Catch Yourself: Virgin. Whore. Virgin. Whore. If you had to pick one to describe yourself, which would it be? The correct answer is neither. These were the two choices available to women for centuries: be chaste, virtuous, innocent, and untouched, or let your libido loose and suffer the fate of the outcast.

The bad girl is neither wildly promiscuous nor woefully repressed. She's rewriting history. She doesn't publicly declare her virginity, nor does she apologize for having a string of past lovers. And she doesn't treat sex like taxes—either it's withheld or she pays up.

Regain Your Footing: Don't let your sexual behavior define you; you are a multifaceted woman.

Freefall #4: You have to be in love to enjoy sex.

Catch Yourself: Many women (but very few men) equate love with great sex. The truth is, love and lust don't always come in the same package. Most of us have male friends we love dearly, but we'd never sleep with them. And we've all lusted after men we hardly knew. Even happily married couples have a hard time maintaining the passion that first brought them together as the years go by and the responsibilities pile up.

Regain Your Footing: Chemistry and infatuation can be the driving factors in a very satisfying sexual relationship that may or may not grow into love. So enjoy the lust while it lasts!

Freefall #5: All feminists are lesbians.

Catch Yourself: We know that you may think this is a ridiculous statement, but believe it or not, there are those who link the two. For some strange reason, they think that any woman who wants equal opportunity and respect is having sex with other women. Go figure. Feminism is not a sexual identity. After all, men can be feminists too. You might want to point that out to the next ignoramus who labels you a "lesbian feminist" because you gave him a piece of your mind.

Regain Your Footing: Only people who feel threatened will hurl a label at you. If you buy into their ignorance, you're selling yourself short.

Beauty

Freefall #1: You have to be skinny and petite to be desirable.

Catch Yourself: Many, many women of all body types are desirable to their partners. Whether you are shapely, medium-sized, big-boned, voluptuous, or large, you *are* sexy and desirable. Don't let magazines, television, Hollywood, peers, or strangers convince you otherwise. That skinniness is next to godliness is some random warped value that has permeated society. But the truth is, we've heard many men say they want their women to have bumps and curves. After all, who wants to sleep with a bag of bones? It is only recently that the waiflike body type is in vogue. At the height of her sex symbol status, Marilyn Monroe weighed 145 pounds and was a size 12.

Regain Your Footing: Remember that sexy can take any form.

Freefall #2: You have to have a perfect body to be worthwhile.

Catch Yourself: First of all, who decides what's perfect? Is there some perfect body committee that defines a perfect body? If you are basing your worth on your body, you are selling yourself short. What defines your value is your intelligence, intuition, wit, creativity, capabilities, hobbies, gifts, talents, perceptions, family and home life, spiritual life, emotional literacy, professional life, academic achievements, creative endeavors, artistic pursuits, and volunteer work. Remember that your body is one one-hundredth of your value.

Regain Your Footing: If you define your worth by your physical body, you are missing a huge piece of who you are and what you bring to this world.

Practice expanding the definition of what makes you worthwhile.

Freefall #3: You'd be happier if you looked like a movie star or a supermodel.

Catch Yourself: Beautiful women are not happier women. They're just, well, beautiful according to societal standards. You see, the more attractive a woman is, the less likely that she'll get positive feedback about what's really special about her. Most beautiful women are trapped by this. They get as caught up in their goddesslike appearance as we do, investing way too much time in looking gorgeous only to find that their physical assets diminish over time.

Regain Your Footing: Beauty fades, but the spirit doesn't. Feed your spirit and you will blossom for many years to come.

Freefall #4: Women grow older; men grow more distinguished.

Catch Yourself: Come on! Men don't have the corner on aging with grace. Sorry, but we don't buy into the myth that all women over fifty are hags while their male counterparts remain hotties. Just look around and you'll see lots of gorgeous women over fifty: Lena Horne, Naomi Judd, Susan Sarandon,

Diahann Carroll, Connie Chung, Charlayne Hunter-Gault, Oprah Winfrey, Debbie Allen, Diane Keaton, Meryl Streep, Twyla Tharp, Peggy Fleming, Althea Gibson, Amy Tan, and Terry McMillan, just to name a few. They're sexy and gorgeous—not because they've had plastic surgery, but because they're doing amazing things with their lives!

Regain Your Footing: Live your life to the fullest and you'll find there's beauty at every age.

The Good Wife and Mother

Freefall #1: Behind every great man is a great woman.

Catch Yourself: Although it's true that many men succeed because they have great female partners, we don't find this saying very empowering. The message behind it is that women should play a supporting role in the lives of men rather than carving out an existence for themselves. While men dream, hope, plan, and struggle, women should be their sounding boards and cheerleaders. Come on! Both men and women owe it to themselves to reach their potential. To do this we all need someone to encourage us—it's not a woman's job.

Regain Your Footing: You'll go crazy if you suppress or undervalue your dreams while bolstering someone else's. If people seek you out for your advice and support, you possess very valuable gifts. Don't let them be abused.

Freefall #2: Married women are happier than single women.

Catch Yourself: Guess again. According to a World Health Organization report from 1996 on women worldwide, married women with children had a higher risk for depression than did married childless women, single women, or single or married men. University of London researchers found that single women typically have fewer mental health issues. Who wouldn't have mental health issues while calling on clients when morning sickness calls on you, brokering deals while pumping breast milk, giving a presentation with leaky breasts, or preparing an urgent memo while your child throws a temper tantrum? Xanax to go with your cabernet, anyone?

Regain Your Footing: Marriage isn't a one-way ticket to nirvana.

Freefall #3: If your house is a mess, it reflects poorly on you.

Catch Yourself: Who cares? Stop buying into the myth that a clean house is a priority and that it's your responsibility. How about letting everyone else do their part? We know it's hard to let this one go, but do you really want to spend so much time cleaning your house? Isn't there something else you'd rather be doing?

Regain Your Footing: Set realistic standards for cleaning and then share the work with your family. Better yet, pay someone to do it for you!

Freefall #4: You must have kids to be truly fulfilled.

Catch Yourself: It's true that children can be deeply satisfying and can open your heart and teach you about love in a profound way. It is also true that women have achieved great success and have found meaning, satisfaction, and love without ever having children. Some notable women include Oprah Winfrey, Ellen DeGeneres, Bonnie Raitt, Diane Sawyer, Kathryn Hepburn, Georgia O'Keefe, Mary Cassatt, Annie Oakley, Frida Kahlo, Joan of Arc, Harriet Tubman, Ella Fitzgerald, and Emily Dickinson.

For many women, it is difficult to determine whether the baby longing is coming from dreams, hormones, or societal messages. Especially when the biological clock starts tick-tocking loudly and a woman's ovaries send red alert messages to her brain (use us or lose us), knowing whether she truly wants to reproduce is a bit perplexing.

If you are grappling with this issue, take plenty of time to read books, and talk it over with loved ones as well as child-free and child-full people. It is not the only path to fulfillment or love. If you want to shower love on a little helpless being but don't want to procreate, remember that little creatures come in all shapes and sizes. And you can always love OPC (other people's children), which enables you to (a) return them when they're going ballistic over a dirty diaper, (b) walk away from projectile spit-up incidents, (c) get restorative sleep on a regular basis, and (d) do whatever you want, whenever you want. (This last point is why parents are envious of child-free folks.)

Regain Your Footing: Having children is a choice, not an obligation or a sure path to fulfillment.

Undecided about kids? Check out the Roll the Ovary activity at the end of this chapter.

The Domestic Goddess Meltdown

Though you were born a mere mortal, your toilet scrubbing, kitchen floor mopping, and diaper changing may have turned you into a real-life goddess—a household deity, a home and garden fixture—without your even knowing. Not sure if you've reached this enlightened state? Let's find out.

1. Do you spend about thirty-five hours a week on housework while your partner clocks only half of that?

2. Do you shoulder most of the responsibility for raising the children, dealing with child care, keeping the house in order, and doing the meal planning?
3. Do you feel as if keeping your family's domestic life running smoothly is primarily your responsibility and your partner is being noble when he pitches in?
4. Do you need to have a meltdown before you get any help?

If you answered yes to any of the above, you are indeed a domestic goddess. Unfortunately, this is one of the lesser goddesses—you don't get to rule the world or shape-shift on a whim. Your life looks more like this: You carry the weight of the household on your shoulders, the weight gets too heavy, you break under the pressure, you melt down, your husband or partner responds to your meltdown, the pressure is relieved momentarily, you feel supported, and you forget the pattern until the next meltdown.

If this has happened over the course of months or years, it is time to put an end to it. Leave your goddesslike ways behind and ask for help—loudly! Then negotiate with your partner what chores each of you will do and stick to it. (The sticking to it is the hard part. If he isn't as good as you at cleaning toilets or folding laundry, you have to let it go—or risk future meltdowns.)

Bad girls don't let themselves get into the meltdown pattern or, if they see it emerging, they put an end to it quickly. Meltdowns rob you of your vitality and energy. Perhaps you like the drama queen bit; if so, save it for the stage, not the living room. Meltdowns and your domestic life don't have to go hand-in-hand. So, have you learned your lessons? Take the *Bad Girl Quiz* at the end of this chapter to find out. Read each question and then circle yes, no, or sometimes.

Freefall #5: Children will bring you happiness.

Catch Yourself: They'll also bring you frustration, anger, hurt, and longing. Children can be a wonderful addition to your life, but they are not responsible for your happiness. You are. If you rely on them to make you happy, you will not only be disappointed but also drive them away.

Regain Your Footing: You must find your own happiness and not depend on your children (or anyone else) to do it for you.

Freefall #6: If you really want a baby, you should just have one and it will all work out.

Catch Yourself: Having kids and starting our own families is something most women and men want. It's part of the natural course of life. But before you decide to do this—with or without a partner—you should consider some cold, hard facts:

1. After having children, you can expect a decrease in your earning power. The main reason for this is that many women decide to work part-time, take a less demanding position, or quit their jobs after having children.

2. Working mothers are changing this, but some employers may take you less seriously when you get pregnant. They may place you on the "mommy track" and deny you raises or promotions, or not assign you to important projects. Of course, this is illegal, but mommy tracking is all too common.

3. You will probably be the child's primary caretaker even if you have a partner and both of you are working full-time. So ask yourself, Am I ready to take on another full-time job and essentially work around the clock?

4. Your free time and spending money will disappear. There'll be less time to sleep, you'll miss days of work when your child is sick, you'll spend lots of money on day care and baby-sitting, and there's no end to all the things your child will want and need.

Regain Your Footing: Plan, plan, plan. If having a family is your dream, know what to expect and plan for it. Hoping that everything will work out won't make it so.

Power

Freefall #1: Women can quietly wield power and influence by "working behind the scenes."

Catch Yourself: No, they can't. Being indirect is not an effective way to speak up, effect change, or make a difference. It also leads to very little positive outcome and may even contribute to serious ailments and disease such as depression, cancer, and alcoholism.

Regain Your Footing: Be direct, not demure.

Freefall #2: Aggressiveness is unattractive in a woman.

Catch Yourself: Says who? Chances are that it is unattractive to people who are threatened by women who have healthy self-esteem and tons of confidence. Do you care about pleasing those people? (The correct answer is *no*.) Being bold and taking action is how you get what you want in this world.

Regain Your Footing: Go full steam ahead into the future of your dreams.

Freefall #3: You shouldn't challenge authority.

Catch Yourself: You may be at risk of being labeled a troublemaker or you might cause a disturbance in an otherwise peaceful relationship, but you have to challenge authority when your happiness is at stake. Why accommodate and "keep the peace" when you can command your own life? Taking charge of your life means you have to lead. Don't give away the power to make decisions about your life to your boss, your partner, your teachers, or your parents. Hey, this is *your* life! Who's in charge here?

Regain Your Footing: Until you lead, you will be living someone else's life.

Freefall #4: You can't be simultaneously feminine and powerful.

Catch Yourself: It's true that some women have made it to the top by mimicking men in appearance and style. But at what price? Being a bad girl means that you can be both powerful and feminine. You don't have to trade one for the other. And you can define femininity in whatever way you wish. You can be sensual, sensitive, sexy, and stylish while being assertive, firm, and determined to get what you want. No two women are alike—create your own formula for success.

Regain Your Footing: You don't have to look and act like a man to be powerful. Be true to yourself.

Freefall #5: Sexual harassment is a thing of the past.

Catch Yourself: Regrettably, sexual harassment is still alive and well. Sure, harassers have wised up and usually stick to verbal harassment that they consider "just joking around." But harassers are still out there. The subtle verbal harassers say things like "I'll bet you've got a date every night" or "You should wear skirts more often." The more obvious harassers say things like "Ever consider selling naked pictures of yourself on the Internet?"

There are nonverbal harassers, too. They stare—not casually glance—at your boobs or your butt when you're trying to have a conversation. Or they steal a wink at a buddy when you're talking to them. And then there's the group that didn't get the memo about being discreet—they don't know there are *laws* against this behavior. They still think it's okay to act on impulse. They're the ones who will grab your ass or put your hand on their crotch "'cause they thought you were attracted to them." Believe it or not, the crotch incident happened to Ann at work. She wishes she had slapped the married man with four children; instead she said, "It's a bit too small for my taste." (For more sassy comebacks, see Trail #7.)

Regain Your Footing: Know the behavior and take action as soon as you see it. If you think it's safe, confront the harasser. If not, get support. Talk to your boss (unless he's the harasser) or your human resources manager.

Work

Freefall #1: Women help other women succeed.

Catch Yourself: Some do, some don't. Unfortunately, some of us don't believe in ourselves, so when we see other women doing well, we feel . . . unsettled. We may feel threatened by women we perceive to have greater gifts than us: more beauty, charm, intelligence, wit, or creativity. Instead of appreciating their wonders, we may subtly challenge them or call their competence into question, hoping to cut them down a notch. Come on, girls! When we sabotage other women, we're tearing apart our own support system. The more women support each other, the better off we'll all be. Let's create a bad girls' network that rivals the good-old boys' network!

Regain Your Footing: Stop sabotaging and start mentoring.

Freefall #2: You'd be happier if you didn't have to work.

Catch Yourself: No, you wouldn't. You'd be happier if you were doing work you loved. We realize it can be very, *very* tough to make a living doing what you love, but that's what we're shooting for. Sure, we all want to quit our day jobs and some of us will. Take your life's work seriously and spend as much time as you can doing what energizes and inspires you.

Regain Your Footing: Doing work you love allows you to build a place for yourself in the world.

Freefall #3: Women can't make decisions.

Catch Yourself: We're always amazed that anyone believes this. Women can't make decisions, but they can raise the next generation, run a household, and build a career in their spare time? Wow, who knew that such critical work could be accomplished in the absence of decision making? Women may deliberate or collaborate more when making decisions—we often construct the big picture from lots of scraps of information. Women, girls, this is an incredible skill we have. Most men eliminate details when making decisions—they just can't manage all the information. But we can. So there's a very good chance that women are better at reaching conclusions and make better decisions.

Regain Your Footing: Don't buy into this nonsense. You can and do make major decisions every day, so if your dream is to run the world or a Fortune 500 company, just do it!

Freefall #4: Women have as much clout in the workplace as men.

Catch Yourself: Unfortunately, they still don't. Barely any women are in executive positions, women are still paid less than men doing the same work with the same degree of experience, a woman's job performance is often judged more harshly than a man's, and women's opinions and decisions are much more likely to be challenged. Don't believe us? Have you counted the number of female heads of religious institutions, governments, or businesses lately? Last time we checked, the pope was male, Congress was a sea of suits and ties, and General Electric's former CEO Jack Welch was the man with the plan.

Regain Your Footing: Be as arrogant and confident as most men are.

When Retro Is Not Cool: The Mommy Track

The year is 2007, or is it 1957? Frankly, there are days when we just can't tell. Everywhere we turn, another brilliant, creative woman is throwing in the towel and becoming a throwback by "choosing" the mommy track. When did it become an attractive option for intelligent, creative, educated women to sign up for full-time mommyhood instead of balancing work and family? Sure we know (secondhand) that it's tough to go to work when you're sleep deprived and leaking breast milk, but when the teeth come in and the training pants come off, isn't it time to get back to our other work in some capacity? And if we don't, doesn't that make us babies?

Oh, sure, we can hear it now. You're not moms, so what do you know about how tough it is? Our answer: *Wah!* You sound like a baby. Tough, you say? Is that the only obstacle—it's tough? Maybe we're not moms, but don't dismiss our tirade. Instead, ponder this: What exactly is the point of the thirty years (plus or minus a few) leading up to reproduction? Are we preparing to be mommies? Last time we checked, we'd left Betty Crocker and *Good Housekeeping* behind and taken up the struggle for equal lives, equal development as human beings, and equal status in the society at large and in our families. How equal is it for men to enjoy careers *and* the fulfillment and joy of being daddies, while we limit our identity and job options to "mommy"? Doesn't that mean we've given up the fight—that we're settling for less than full equality?

Although Carol is not a mom, her mom, Margo, taught her a thing or two. Carol grew up in an Irish Catholic suburb of Boston, where most families had at least five kids, and most moms were housewives—but not Mrs. Brunelli. While her five kids were young, she worked part-time—often at night—to keep her nursing career on track, knowing that one day she could go at it full throttle. This was not the case with the other neighborhood moms. They were voracious consumers of nicotine and caffeine, who appeared to be junkies—at least to a young, impressionable child of the '70s. They were slovenly, unkempt, and sluggish (despite the mass ingestion of stimulants). Their houses overflowed with sticky dishes and dirty clothes, and discarded toys lay in piles everywhere. Their kids were runny-nosed, unruly, and seemingly running wild. Had a documentary been made of their lives, it would have been titled something like *Moms on Uppers: A Cautionary Tale* or *To Hell and Back: Housewives Scare Girls into Getting a Job and Getting a Life.*

While the Brunellis' home was not immaculate—the kids, a dog, and an occasional guinea pig made sure of that—it was hygienic and orderly. The children were not perfect, but the parents were definitely running the place (probably because the kids were given chores, which distracted them from being holy terrors). And while Margo's life may sound daunting to the 2007 mom—who has five kids anymore?—it was simply what Margo did. It worked out amazingly well. She carved out an impressive (high-paying) career, and her kids stayed out of jail and stayed in college.

So before you accept the full-time mommy job offer, consider this: The choices we make matter to all women. What we do or do not do sets a precedent for future generations. (Do we really want to go back in time?) And don't we all want our girls to grow up to be the president of the United States instead of the first lady?

BAD GIRL QUIZ

1. I work harder than most of my coworkers.
   - a. Yes
   - b. No
   - c. Sometimes
2. I don't feel complete without a partner.
   - a. Yes
   - b. No
   - c. Sometimes
3. I often regret not saying what I really think.
   - a. Yes
   - b. No
   - c. Sometimes
4. I promote my accomplishments at work.
   - a. Yes
   - b. No
   - c. Sometimes
5. I believe a woman's life can be fulfilling with or without children.
   - a. Yes
   - b. No
   - c. Sometimes
6. I love my job (paid or unpaid).
   - a. Yes
   - b. No
   - c. Sometimes
7. I make an effort to mentor other women.
   - a. Yes
   - b. No
   - c. Sometimes
8. I sometimes have meltdowns before asking for help with domestic chores.
   - a. Yes
   - b. No
   - c. Sometimes
9. I think women lose value as they age.
   - a. Yes
   - b. No
   - c. Sometimes
10. I often defer to men when making decisions.
    - a. Yes
    - b. No
    - c. Sometimes

11. Thin women are happier than stocky women.

    a. Yes   b. No   c. Sometimes

12. I'd be happier if I didn't have to work.

    a. Yes   b. No   c. Sometimes

Answers:

1. a. 0 , b. 2, c. 1	7. a. 2, b. 0, c. 1
2. a. 0, b. 2, c.1	8. a. 0, b. 2 c. 1
3. a. 0, b. 2, c. 1	9. a. 0, b. 2, c. 1
4. a. 2, b. 0, c. 1	10. a. 2, b. 0, c. 1
5. a. 2, b. 0, c. 1	11. a. 0, b. 2, c. 1
6. a. 2, b. 0, c. 1	12. a. 0, b. 2, c. 1

What was your score and what does it mean? Well, the bigger your score, the badder the bad girl. Find out where you fall in the bad girl scale.

Bad Girl Scale

24 Only!	Stiletto Girl
18–23	Platform Girl
12–17	Wedge Girl
6–11	Cuban Girl
0–5	Kitten Girl

Regaining Your Footing

What freefalls have you taken? How did you catch yourself and regain your footing?

Freefall #1:
How I Regained My Footing:
Freefall #2:
How I Regained My Footing:

Roll the Ovary

Play Roll the Ovary! We're not claiming that this table will be the deciding factor in your decision-making process, but it will get the ovary rolling, or not. Look at each column and determine if the statements apply to you. Then score that column.

Womanly Duty	Gripped by Hormones	Dream Come True
You've never had an affinity for children, but you feel like you should emulate Mother Theresa in the kid department.	You're single and during ovulation, you start shopping at the supermarket for fathers for your unconceived child.	You've always seen yourself as a mother. When you imagine morning sickness, you envision bliss.
You think children are little urchins that should be sent away to a	When you visualize menopause, you anticipate grieving over the loss of the	You can't wait to coddle, nurture, wipe noses and bottoms, educate

deserted island with no boat, but your parents want grandkids.	monthly fertility ritual.	little people and answer the "why" questions.
You love your child-free life, but your partner wants to see if his swimmers can get the prize.	During your period, you stress out over the lack of meaning in your life. You need a meaning-of-life delivery device, and you think a child is the answer.	You'll still feel the love after 1,825 peanut butter sandwiches and 4,380 diaper changes and that's just for one kid. (Multiply by the number of kids for accurate totals.)
If you answered yes 2-3 times, do not roll; you'll lose the game. Once, go to Dream Come True.	If you answered yes 2-3 times, think about kids when you're not hormonal. Once, go to Dream Come True. If you answered no 3 times, do not roll.	If you answered yes 1-3 times, roll and you'll win! If you answered no 3 times; do not roll; you'll lose the game.

Girlfriends Forever

Another myth we'd like to dispel is that all women are catty, cunning, and competitive—basically, out to get one another. Please! Most of us look to our girl-friends to get us through the day, the latest crisis, or a major life change. We form deep, caring relationships that last a lifetime.

1. Write down the name of the first girlfriend who pops into your mind.

   _____

2. What do you love about her? What does she give you that no one else does?

   _____
   _____
   _____
   _____
   _____

Luscious Body Hot Springs

I've had a little lipo. I've had a little Botox. And you know what? None of it works. None of it.
—Jamie Lee Curtis

About This Trail: Free your mind and your body will follow.

Duration: You'll be on this trail for as long as it takes to let go of calorie counting, body shame, fad diets, and love-based weight loss.

Distance: When you stop focusing on changing your body and start focusing on changing the world, this trail will be a walk in the park.

Difficulty: Until you apply the trail tips, you'll feel as if you're on a StairMaster to hell.

Elevation: This trail can take you to heights never before imagined. Your spirit will soar when your body stops weighing you down.

Backpack Essentials: Life dreams, weed whacker (to weed out the bad body thoughts), basic math skills, passion and persistence, return on investment formula, and a tankful of self-esteem.

What to Leave Behind: Barbie, Botox, boob jobs, bad boyfriends, binging, and berating.

Early Pitfalls: Buy into heroin-addict chic and you'll never get past the trailhead.

Trail Tip: If you feel discouraged, remind yourself that your body is your temple. Luscious Body Hot Springs awaits you.

At the Trail's End: On this trail you will discover that as you shift your focus away from your body to your mind, you'll set yourself free. Bad girls don't get caught up in a trail of tears over body image. If you quiet the messages both inside and out, you'll learn that your body is perfect as it is.

Imagine soaking in a clear pool of steaming mineral water on the banks of a rushing river. As you soak in the mineral water underneath a canopy of stars, you have a sense that your body is as it should be—beautiful, natural, and sensual. The curves and lines are perfectly executed as if a master designer custom-made your body just for you.

Learn how to infuse Luscious Body Hot Springs into your daily life. The basic trail tip is to free your mind, and your body will follow. We're asking you to consider a paradox—if you take away the focus from your body, you will start to see that your body is perfect exactly as it is.

Start by asking yourself, Would I rather count calories or change the world? The answer seems obvious, but the truth is that many women spend their days counting calories, chastising themselves for consuming too many, or berating their uncooperative body parts. Don't believe us? Check this out:

- An estimated one in three of all dieters develops compulsive dieting attitudes and behaviors. Of these, one-quarter will develop full or partial eating disorders.
- An estimated one in one hundred American women binges and purges to lose weight (that's approximately 2.5 million women).
- Anorexia afflicts as many as one in every one hundred girls and young women.
- An estimated 10 percent of female college students suffer from a clinical or subclinical (borderline) eating disorder, of which over half suffer from bulimia nervosa.
- 15 percent of young women have significantly disordered eating attitudes and behavior.
- Each day, Americans spend an average of $109 million on dieting and diet-related products.
- Between elementary and high school, the percentage of girls in the United States who are "happy with the way I am" drops from 60 percent to 29 percent.
- 80 percent of ten-year-old American girls diet.
- The number one magic wish for young girls ages eleven to seventeen is to be thinner.

A Thanksgiving tale illustrates our point. Bridget was at her family's Thanksgiving celebration. Her stepsister,

Lilly, and her husband were hosting the event. They have two exuberant, gifted daughters and a tightly knit extended family. After the meal was served, Lilly's mom requested that the family members go around the table and share what they were thankful for. People gave thanks for their loved ones and health, for good fortune and exciting opportunities. Then it was Lilly's turn. She gave thanks for the fact that on this day, she could eat carbs. Bridget nearly dropped the bowl of candied yams she was passing. Was Lilly so starved for carbs that her brain wasn't functioning correctly and this was the best contribution she could make? Or was this truly the thing she was most thankful for?

Counting calories and obsessing over our weight, imperfect bodies, and inability to lose ten pounds in ten days is a miserable and pointless way to spend our time and energy. So why do we do it? Because we like to be miserable? Because we want our lives to be pointless? No and no. Because it's part of our culture; it's part of our everyday lives.

Below are some comments we've heard. These messages plant seeds of discontent that can lead to body consciousness, obsession, or worse—eating disorders.

- She's got a pretty face; too bad she's not thinner.
- She'd better lose weight or she'll never get a man.
- She's got junk in her trunk.
- She doesn't look as good as she did a few years ago.

- What's with her boobs? They look like mosquito bites.
- Why would she get pregnant and ruin that perfect body?
- She looks great; she doesn't look pregnant at all!
- Women with eating disorders are nice to look at.

This is the background noise we hear as we go about our daily lives. There's no escape from the messages that remind us we're not the sexy sirens we're supposed to be; they permeate the airwaves and print media.

These messages have a powerful shrinking effect on our self-esteem and our bodies. You've undoubtedly noticed over the past decade that women have been steadily dwindling. Even Victoria's Secret models, once voluptuous and curvaceous, are now anorexics with breast implants. Tomatoes on toothpicks. Fashion and most women's magazines convey the message that anything above a size six is too large; four is the new six; two is the new four; and zero is really the ideal. It's good to have juicy lips, inflated breasts, and a perky butt, but the rest of you should look like a heroin addict. Now actresses are getting cheek implants, Botox injections, collagen in their lips, and eyebrow lifts. Excuse me, but why is it a good thing to have high eyebrows? So your face is in a permanent state of surprise? Is this procedure giving a new meaning to high-brow and low-brow? And to be simultaneously swollen from collagen and frozen from Botox must be incredibly uncomfortable. But who cares about comfort when you have to reach unattainable beauty standards? Nipped, tucked, lifted, cut, frozen, injected, and swollen—what is going on? Has everyone lost their minds?

We've received body image messages ever since we were girls that tell us our worth resides in our bodies. In adolescence, we learn to measure our self-worth by the size of our budding breasts, the absence of body fat, and by others' responses to our sex appeal.

Here's a story that illustrates this point. Alexi, an eleven-year-old girl, was looking with disdain at a magazine photo of Jessica Simpson, deemed Hollywood's best body. Her mother asked her what was wrong. Alexi said, "She so doesn't have the best body. She's fat." Jessica Simpson is anything but fat.

Her mother responded with concern by trying to correct her daughter's budding body image distortion. Her husband said, "You're just upset because she insulted you."

She snapped at her husband, who had missed the point. "This is precisely how eating disorders begin," she told him.

Alexi's father is part of the problem.

Free Your Mind and Your Body Will Follow

Where did women's body obsession come from? In the past, many women had little or no earning power and few assets. If women didn't marry, they would likely be ostracized and destitute—cast out of society. Women would become old maids, a fate worse than death. The other choices available to women were to become nuns or prostitutes.

If the old maid, nun, or prostitute options weren't appealing, women had to attract a man and that required maximizing sex appeal—rosy cheeks, pouty lips, child-bearing hips, voluptuous breasts, a small waist, and slender legs. Women's power resided in their bodies.

Times have changed. Women in Western countries don't have to attract a man to survive. So why are we stuck in this outmoded way of thinking? Because it takes time for worldviews, assumptions, and beliefs to shift. Our thinking needs to catch up with the times. We must remove the corsets constricting our brains, and fling them off. We should remind ourselves that we can survive—even thrive—without a man. We can have whatever body is best for us.

Free your mind and your body will follow. But how do you free your mind? By observing limiting thoughts and redirecting your brain power in more constructive ways. If you find yourself thinking about how your body rates or doesn't rate, you are most likely involved in self-loathing and shame; you are keeping yourself small. When women keep themselves small, they don't realize their power or potential; they don't go forth and change the world.

Imagine if Elizabeth Cady Stanton had been paralyzed by shame over her expanding waistline, rather than helping women win the right to vote. What if Margaret Sanger had been focused on obtaining perfect abs instead of helping women gain universal access to birth control? What if Rosa Parks didn't eat carbs, and was dreaming of mashed potatoes rather than of equality for African Americans?

Think about all the collective creative feminine energy and potential that has been wasted on counting calories, restricting, binging, shaming, and despising our bodies. Think of all the poems, plays, and novels that could have been written; the symphonies, choruses, and songs that could have been composed; the sculptures and paintings created; the social change enacted; the policies implemented; and the companies started if only it weren't for the business of counting calories. If only we could be happy or even just satisfied with our bodies, we would be free to change the world with our creative and intellectual expression.

By turning inward and focusing on our defects and imperfections, we are denying the world of our unique contributions. We don't have to be perfect looking or acting to contribute and create. We don't have to look like Malibu Barbie before our lives can begin. They can start right now—whether we're shaped like a pear, a strawberry, an apple, a butternut squash, or a carrot. All are delicious.

Even more important, we have to eat to create. When we're starving, we can't contribute. Ever notice that when you're depriving yourself of the calories you need, your mind vacates and you can't perform the simplest tasks? We call this the cognitive deficit zone. This just won't do if we're going to run the world. We need to eat well to lead, direct, create, run, leap, sing, dance, paint, sculpt, play, and make love.

Consider this. Would you rather:

- Gaze at your butt in the mirror or watch cloud formations overhead?
- Shop for clothes that are slimming or finish a home improvement project?
- Calculate daily calories or learn about investing for your future?
- Chastise yourself over not having the perfect body or call a beloved old friend?
- Read the latest fad diet book or get lost in a great piece of literature?

- Spend hundreds of dollars on diet bars and drinks or add to your music collection?
- Worry about the size of your thighs or the size of your helping hand?
- Obsess over your dress size or the size of your paycheck?
- Read all the labels on your food or teach an illiterate person to read?
- Worry about the enormity of your hips or the magnitude of your spirit?

So you may be wondering, what is a bad girl's relationship to food? Does she throw off all restrictions and eat with abandon? Glazed donuts at the office? Fried cheesesteaks for lunch? Tuxedo cheesecake for dinner? Funnel cakes on the weekend? Sorry, no. But you also don't have to eat kale, tofu, and seaweed every day to be a bad girl.

A bad girl eats for sustenance and treats herself from time to time. And when she treats herself, she does not chastise, criticize, or analyze herself. Most important, bad girls don't gobble their emotions or swallow their dreams. What good are feelings and dreams broken down by digestive enzymes?

When you think you're hungry, did you ever stop to think that you might be hungry for something other than food? Although it is a simple act to fill yourself with comfort food (chocolate, ice cream, potato chips), does it really bring you comfort? Or just more pain, agony, guilt, regret, and self-loathing? Food is usually not the answer to pain, anger, grief, boredom, low self-esteem, anxiety, and loneliness.

Food eaten when you're not hungry is often a failure of imagination. But it's not your fault. Living in a consumer society, we reach for quick fixes and instant gratification. We're encouraging you to be a bad girl and try to understand your void—the emptiness you feel that masquerades as hunger.

Bad girls figure out what they're hungry for and fill the void, not with chocolate raspberry mousse or mocha cream, but with a filler that matches the hunger. Take a look at the Filling the Void table.

Filling the Void

Hunger	Filler
To be intellectually stimulated	Work on a crossword puzzle or Sudoku
To express your emotions	Write about your feelings in a journal or share them with a friend, partner, or therapist
To connect socially	Plan a coffee date, join a book club, participate in Stitch and Bitch (a knitting club), or schedule regular walks with a friend

To be creative	Create a collage, write a song, choreograph a dance, Photoshop your favorite photo, or design a logo or a website
To be physically active	Try Pilates, swing or salsa dance, yoga, rock climbing, telemark skiing, or the circus arts (trapeze!)
To boost your self-esteem	Take risks (scare yourself every day!), try new things, set goals and visualize dreams (in detail)
To contribute to the community	Volunteer with a retirement community, an AIDS organization, an arts alliance, drug/alcohol abuse program, homeless shelter, or the community food bank
To be heard	Speak your mind at a meeting of a support group or club, create a blog or respond to someone else's, write a letter to the editor, or call into a radio show
To be touched	Get a massage, shiatsu cranial-sacral therapy, pedicure, manicure
To have solitude	Meditate at home or by a stream or lake, hike in nature, take a bubble bath, soak in mineral hot springs, sit on your back porch at night and take in the stars and moon

Women make choices every day about how to spend time and energy. Women not only waste time on body image obsession, but they also waste their hard-earned cash. We have created a Return on Investment (ROI) table that presents popular cosmetic surgery options and offers alternatives that are more beneficial.

A few years ago, many of us thought cosmetic surgery was only for aging actresses with sagging faces, but the democratization of cosmetic procedures has begun. On TV, we see average-looking people transformed into supermodels after spending a few hours under the knife. We may find ourselves looking with disdain at a less-than-ideal body part, thinking: *a little nip or tuck or enhancement couldn't hurt.*

Back to the ROI table. You may find that the ROI on some of these body-altering procedures is capturing a sugar daddy, in which case a financial return is achieved. However, there is no guarantee that injecting poison, implanting water balloons, stretching your face, or sucking the fat out of your body will land you a trophy wife gig. Given that, we think your money would be better spent in other ways.

Return on Investment

Cosmetic Alteration	Cost	End Result	Better ways to spend your money	End Result
Botox	$300 each area injected every 6 months	Frozen face—minimizing wrinkles	• iPod • Car • Everyday luxuries	• Music to your ears • Wheels to travel • Adding zest to life

Boob job	$8,000	Bigger boobs	• Down payment on a house • Health or life insurance • Home improvement	• Home ownership • Being prepared for the unexpected • Making your house a home
Tummy tuck	$6,000	Flat abs	• Timeshare in a tropical locale • Pay off debt • Invest in bonds	• Relaxation and umbrella drinks • Guilt-free living • Money for the future
Face lift	$8,500	A tight face	• World travel • Landscaping • Adopt a child from a Third World country	• Memories • Blossoms and beauty • Enhance your family
Liposuction	$6,000	Fat removed	• A pet plus pet care and food for six months • Hire a house cleaner/nanny	• Countless years of unconditional love • More leisure time

Rather than using your math skills to calculate calorie intake and output and calorie burn, we suggest that you use numbers in a different way. We've come up with a trail tip that will help you progress on the Luscious Body Hot Springs trail. It's called Body Fat Math. Body Fat Math is a lesson in how *not* to live your life obsessing over every morsel that passes your lips or every body part that doesn't fit an ideal image seen in an airbrushed magazine ad. Not every woman needs this lesson. Let's see if you do.

- Do you obsess about what you've eaten, what you're going to eat, and how you're going to work it off when you do eat it?
- Do you regularly inventory the body parts you're unhappy with or wish you looked like someone else?
- Have you ever decided you would lose ten pounds by a specific date and then run out and spent hard-earned cash on diet shakes and bars?
- Do you spend most of the day thinking about what you can't eat and feeling miserable because of it?

If you answered yes to any of these questions, you need the Body Fat Math trail tip. Now, don't shift into math anxiety mode. It's a myth that women can't do math. And this doesn't require calculating square roots or solving algebraic equations. It's simple addition.

The objective of this trail tip is twofold: (1) You'll determine how much time and money you spend obsessing over your imperfect body. (2) You'll realize how much time and money you're wasting, and decide to change.

Body Fat Math

What are your triggers? What makes you obsess about your body? Once you've been set off, how much time and money do you spend doing this? Let's find out.

Trigger	What I'm thinking	Time It Takes (minutes/ hours)	Money I spend ($)
Responding to my boyfriend's inquiry: "Have you gained weight?"	I look like shit. He's not attracted to me anymore.	• 120 hours obsessing over my boyfriend's feelings • 6 hours asking for reassurance from my boyfriend • 5 hours finding the perfect pants = 131 hours	$250 on several new pairs of slimming pants.

Passing by the window of a bakery, seeing something yummy, and treating myself to a piece of mocha cheese-cake	I shouldn't have eaten that cheese-cake. Now I'll fast for a week.	168 hours in the cognitive deficit zone = incompetence, dizziness, depression and anxiety	$6.00 for a piece of cheesecake
Bathing suit shopping for summer vaca-tion in two months	I look like a hippo. I must lose at least 15 pounds before I can be seen in public wear-ing a bathing suit.	5 minutes every waking hour until bathing suit season = 80 hours	$600 on Weight Watchers
Spotting hard-bodied girls in ads for weight loss machines and fitness centers	I want to look like those girls.	All the time	$850 per year on a rarely used gym membership
Responding to a big butt comment made by a male coworker	My butt is expanding; pretty soon it will be the complemen-tary shape of a chair.	Every time you see your coworker—10 minutes x 260 days = 40 hours	

Now it's your turn to identify your triggers and the associated thoughts, time, and money spent. Use the table below to write down how much time and money you spend counting calories or obsessing over your body's shape and size.

Trigger	What I'm thinking	Time It Takes (minutes/ hours)	Money I spend ($)

Now do the Body Fat Math.

1. Add up all the time and money you spend in one year counting calories or obsessing over your body.

The answer is: I spend _____ (time) and _____ ($) a year counting calories or obsessing over the shape and size of my body.

2. What would you rather do with this time and money? Check all that apply or make up your own. The important thing is to follow it.

___ Take a long aromatherapy, candlelit bath.

___ Write a short story or a personal essay.

___ Learn watercolor or oil painting.

___ Make a difference in an elderly person's life.

___ Paint accent walls in my home.

___ Learn Italian, Spanish, or Chinese.

___ Spend time with my kids/family/friends.

___ Learn something new and completely impractical (e.g., low-flying trapeze).

___ Get lost in a Nobel Prize–winning novel.

___ Volunteer with Habitat for Humanity or the Humane Society.

___ Get a hot stone or Thai massage.

___ Teach an illiterate adult to read.

___ Throw a gourmet dinner party.

___ Train my dog to be a companion in senior centers or hospitals.

___ Learn a new software program.

___ Plan a rafting or biking adventure.

___Work with a troubled child or adolescent.

BAD GIRL QUIZ

1. I eat whatever I want, but regret it later.
    a. Yes   b. No   c. Sometimes
2. I worry that my partner or potential dates are critical of my body.
    a. Yes   b. No   c. Sometimes
3. I believe that my body is perfect for me.
    a. Yes   b. No   c. Sometimes
4. I think cosmetic surgery would add to the quality of my life.
    a. Yes   b. No   c. Sometimes
5. I think the ideal female body is unattainable.
    a. Yes   b. No   c. Sometimes
6. I think that thinner women are more successful.
    a. Yes   b. No   c. Sometimes
7. I am more concerned with health than body size.
    a. Yes   b. No   c. Sometimes
8. I work out more than two hours a day.
    a. Yes   b. No   c. Sometimes
9. I have an eating disorder or disordered thinking.
    a. Yes   b. No   c. Sometimes
10. I'm aware of how negative body messages affect me.
    a. Yes   b. No   c. Sometimes

11. I think that eating comfort food is counterproductive.

    a. Yes   b. No   c. Sometimes

Answers:

1. a. 0 , b. 2, c. 1	7. a. 2, b. 0, c. 1
2. a. 0, b. 2, c.1	8. a. 0, b. 2 c. 1
3. a. 2, b. 0, c. 1	9. a. 0, b. 2, c. 1
4. a.0, b. 2, c. 1	10. a. 2, b. 0, c. 1
5. a. 2, b. 0, c. 1	11. a. 2, b. 0, c. 1
6. a. 0, b. 2, c. 1	

What was your score and what does it mean? Well, the bigger your score, the badder the bad girl. Find out where you fall in the bad girl scale.

Bad Girl Scale

22 Only!	Stiletto Girl
16–21	Platform Girl
11–15	Wedge Girl
6–10	Cuban Girl
0–5	Kitten Girl

Sabotage Gulch

Niceness is a disease. Luckily, there's a cure.
—Carol Brunelli

About This Trail: If you're afraid of heights, don't look down.

Duration: If you plunge into the gulch, your duration may be a lifetime. If you avoid the gulch, you'll be at the next trail marker by the time you can say "Baby talk is for babies."

Distance: It depends. If you fall into the gulch, the distance triples. If you avoid the gulch, it's an easy ascent with panoramic views.

Difficulty: The trail hugs the gulch with sheer drop-offs. If you don't heed the trail warnings, you may plunge into the gulch and never be discovered.

Elevation: Above the clouds, if you stop sabotaging yourself.

Backpack Essentials: A big horn for tooting, your own fan club, and a sword to slay the doubting demon.

What to Leave Behind: Baby talk, the lady-in-waiting, the damsel in distress, the policy of politeness, sugar and spice and everything nice, disclaimers, and beauty pageants.

Early Pitfalls: Talking or acting like Little Red Riding Hood will summon the Big Bad Wolf from the forest. He'll eat you for lunch.

Trail Tip: Take off your stilettos and stay away from the edge. It's a loooong way down, and nearly impossible to climb out.

At the Trail's End: You'll find that in order to change your life for the better, you're going to have to change yourself. Eliminating baby talk, disclaimers, conversations about your body parts, and other sabotage behavior from your daily routine will free up time and energy to create the life you've always dreamed of.

Do you think the following statements sound more like a man or a woman: Oh, I'm sorry; I really shouldn't have said that. I had no idea what I was talking about in the meeting. The next time, I'll just let you handle it.

What's your best guess? If you answered a woman, you were right. How often have you heard language like this coming from a guy? Most likely, not too often. But for many girls and women, apologizing, using disclaimers, and putting ourselves down is a daily occurrence. If you haven't yet hiked the Sabotage Gulch trail, you are probably doing things every day that sabotage your success and happiness.

Here are some of the things we do to work against ourselves. If you do any of these things, you may want to consider leaving them by the side of the trail, or better yet—chucking them into Sabotage Gulch. As you read through this list ask yourself, what has this behavior done for me lately?

Trail Warning #1: Talking Like a Baby

You've heard women who do this, haven't you? A young woman who had just graduated from Boston University with an advanced degree was having a hard time finding work. After six months she was still desperately searching for a good job that could pay her bills, including hefty student loans. She explained in a baby voice that she couldn't understand why people weren't hiring her; she felt as though people weren't taking her seriously. Think about it: If she presented her accomplishments and rationale for why she's the best candidate for the job in the voice of an eight-year-old, are the interviewers going to listen to her tone or content? Does the voice of an eight-year-old girl inspire confidence in people making a risky hiring decision?

Baby talkers speak in a whispery, high voice as though they're too weak to stand on their own. They come across as if they have no confidence in what they are saying—that they are, in fact, saying nothing. That explains why every statement sounds like a question: "Tomorrow's supposed to be sunny? The capital of Germany is Berlin? My car has an oil leak?"

Baby talkers come in all shapes and sizes, but we've noticed baby talk is especially popular with high school and college-age women. Why are young women doing this and why don't we say something? Perhaps cultivating the goo-goo gab is an attention-getting strategy. But believe us when we say, you don't want guys who are turned on by robbing the cradle. Reserve baby talk for babies. Practice your deep, resonant, powerful voice that emanates from your center; it may be a powerful screening device that chases away creepy dudes on power trips.

Trail Warning #2: Trying to Please, Please, Please

There's no better way for a woman *not* to get ahead in life than to please, please, please. Do everything your parents tell you. Meet all your teachers' and employers' expectations. Anticipate your family's every want and need but never, ever, please yourself.

Have you ever seen that ad on TV about a job site on the Web? It shows one kid after another talking about what they want to be when they grow up. "When I grow up, I want to be a middle manager," says one. "When I grow up, I want to get paid less for doing more." And so it goes. Do most women have such low expectations? Do women remain chaste, do their homework and chores punctually, volunteer for every committee at work and at school, *and* play the domestic goddess because these things are expected of them or because these things please them?

We know that you're not one of these women, but just to be sure, ask yourself, What do I want out of life? What do I want to achieve? What are *my* expectations of *me*?

Trail Warning #3: Taking a Stand without Offending

Taking a stand without offending is like taking a bath without water. Impossible, unless you like lounging around in an empty tub. If you don't take a stand, you probably aren't saying anything that's worth saying. Your message is pure fluff—cotton candy; something for everyone, except you. One thing's for sure: If you take a stand, have an opinion or a point of view, or have a personality, you will offend some people. There's no getting around it. But part of being a bad girl is being able to tolerate some people not liking you—learning to live with the discomfort that people may not agree with your opinions, choices, or approaches. Look at it this way: If a few people don't like you or are taken aback by you, you're probably on the right track. That means you actually have a distinct personality. Don't trade in your personality for popularity. You may be a people pleaser, but the most important person to please is yourself.

Trail Warning #4: Staying Quiet (Not Rocking the Boat)

If you don't speak up, you will not get what you want or deserve and "things" will not change. Ann and Carol have been disappointed with some very intelligent and strong women who just didn't think it was worth their effort to speak up about critical things. They wouldn't ask for more money when they knew male colleagues were making more; they wouldn't speak out when male colleagues were given more perks or when they stepped out of line with "minor" sexual harassment transgressions; they made excuses for their lousy boyfriends and husbands. They kept quiet in order to keep the peace and, guess what? They had no inner peace. In the outside world, nothing changed either.

Think about this: When you speak up about something that is clearly wrong, you help the rest of us, and you contribute to change for the better.

Trail Warning #5: Waiting

Wait for your boss to notice what a great job you're doing *and* give you a raise. Wait for that special someone to call. Wait until you're married or in a committed relationship to buy your own place. Wait until you're a size two to buy that pair of jeans you've had your eye on. Why do many of us patiently wait for life to happen or good things to come to us? Could it be we're buying into good girl myths, or do we just feel unworthy? Think about it this way: If you wait too long, hell could freeze over and you could become an ice sculpture.

Remember, you are worthy; you deserve health, happiness, and new pants that fit! No amount of waiting is going to bring your dreams closer to realization. Stop waiting and start living every day as if it were your last.

Trail Warning #6: Expecting Telepathy

Imagine a world where everyone is pointing a movie camera at themselves. They watch as they smile strategically, say clever things, laugh knowingly, exude competence, feign confidence, and seek admiration and praise. This is our world minus the cameras, with the exception of Hollywood. One thing to keep in mind is that the vast majority of people are busy thinking about themselves; they are not attuned to your needs, wants, and desires. You're lucky if they even notice that you got your hair cut, let alone what your emotional flavor of the day is. They're so caught up in the drama of their own lives, they probably won't notice what you're experiencing. So, that leaves you with two choices when it comes to getting your needs met:

- Expect telepathy from people who probably aren't psychic.
- Ask for what you want and need.

Okay, we realize the first choice wasn't fair, but you get the point. We also realize that being direct about what you need is sometimes uncomfortable. You still may be thinking, If people really loved me, they would know what I wanted. But people can love you and still have no idea what you need. Psychic powers are not a prerequisite for love.

Expecting telepathy is not reasonable. No one knows what you need better than yourself. When you expect telepathy from your lover, partner, friends, family or boss, and you don't get what you need, your resentment will start to build. And build. And build. Then, because no one has read your mind, you explode and say what you needed to say all along—only you say it like a raving lunatic. Things might be hurled across the room, like porcelain elves, Aunt Ethel's china, or duck-billed planters. If both words and objects are flying, which is more likely to get attention? What happens to your message while you're throwing a fit? It is lost. Why not avoid the emotional eruption routine altogether and say what is on your mind before the tension starts to build?

Trail Warning #7: Believing the Doubting Demon

Do you recognize this mind chatter: Am I really the best person for this? Did I say the right thing? I shouldn't have done that. What will they think of me? Why didn't I do that well? I'm not as good as he. I'm an imposter; I really don't know what I'm doing. I don't deserve this promotion/raise/praise. If I were a good mother/wife/daughter, I would have . . .

Think of those thoughts as the voice of the doubting demon within. The doubting demon has one goal: to have you doubting yourself so much that it has complete power over you. The demon undermines your self-confidence and keeps you and others guessing about your competence and abilities. The truth is that everyone has doubts about himself or herself, but some people, especially women, let the voice of doubt take over. Once you give the doubting demon airtime, it gets greedy and wants to seize your cognitive airwaves. The doubting demon won't stop until it has stopped you. Before you know it, you won't even want to go out of your house because the demon has you fooled into thinking that your doubts are real. Your doubts are just thoughts, and thoughts aren't real unless you make them so. Talk back until the doubting demon doubts itself. Figure that one out!

Trail Warning #8: Refusing to Blow Your Own Horn

Who gets more attention in the marching band, a timid flute player or a booming tuba player? Okay, so you may see yourself as a flautist, but for a moment we'd like you to imagine yourself blowing into that tuba above all the other instruments. Imagine yourself as a tuba player when it comes to getting the attention you deserve.

We know that horn blowing doesn't come easily or naturally, especially to those of us who were taught to be quiet, unassuming good girls. Horn blowing may be seen as impolite, brash, brazen, unattractive, aggressive, or arrogant. Yeah. So what? The truth is that refusing to blow your own horn *will* work against you in most cases. People *should* know who deserves credit for a successful project, but the person who will likely get the credit is the one who promotes himself or herself the most tirelessly. Also, if you make yourself visible, you will likely be one of the last to get laid off, if layoffs occur. Make yourself noticeable whether it's comfortable or not. If you are humble, you can still do this. Just make sure the people in your life know how valuable you are! Think unabashed self-promotion. You'll soon learn to bask in your own glory.

Trail Warning #9: Objectifying Yourself

Once in a companywide meeting, a straight-shooting female vice president of a multimillion-dollar health care organization was giving a tough talk about changes that were required for profitability. During this presentation she said, "My not-so-small tusch (Yiddish for "buttocks") is on the line." How was the size of her body part relevant to her message? It wasn't. Drawing attention to her body diminished her credibility. Would a man of an equal or lesser position refer to the size of his body parts to convey his message? No. Why is it that even when we've made it to the top, we still talk about our bottoms?

Trail Warning #10: Using Disclaimers

"I don't really know what I'm talking about. I'm probably confused, so don't take this too seriously, but . . ." Consider the case of Julie. When Julie was a girl, her brilliance was surpassed only by her low opinion of herself. Whenever she participated in class, she would preface her comments with statements such as: "This is probably not going to make any sense, but . . ." or "I have no idea what I'm talking about, but . . ." And then what would follow would be an astute analysis of the topic being discussed. Her body language and disclaimers conveyed extreme self-doubt, even self-loathing, yet her intellectual capabilities were astonishing. Incidentally, she is now a very successful lawyer. She ditched the disclaimers somewhere between torts and habeus corpus.

If you rely on disclaimers as crutches for your limping self-esteem, practice omitting them from your speech. Disclaimers are flashing neon billboards that say doubt me because I doubt myself! To quote a friend's daughter who is a vivacious and self-assured seven-year-old girl: Just believe in yourself—okay?

Trail Warning #11: Avoiding the Imposter Syndrome

What do we mean by this? Most successful people have put themselves out there in business, creative endeavors, or relationships before they felt fully prepared or ready. When you take risks in life, you will often feel like an imposter. The imposter feeling is a sign that you are on the right track; it shows that you are challenging yourself. What's important when feeling like an imposter is to not let it limit what you undertake or stop you in your tracks. You will probably have to experience the imposter syndrome to get to the other side of mastery. Applaud the imposter in you; don't shy away from it. Chances are the woman

almost as if there are a limited number of "sorrys" and women are hoarding them. Let's start sharing the "sorrys" with the fellas.

Do women feel that they have to apologize for their very existence? Think about it this way: Every time beyond the first time you say "I'm sorry" you go into a shrinking machine. Then, with each "I'm sorry" the shrinking machine is activated. After multiple "I'm sorrys" you're literally a shrinking violet, until you're nearly invisible.

The next time you notice a woman or girl overusing "sorry," count the number of times she says it. Then gently remind her that she doesn't have to over-apologize. Saying "I'm sorry" once is enough.

Trail Warning #14: Carrying Your Partner's Emotional Load

Imagine you are climbing a mountain with your life partner. You are hauling an eighty-pound backpack with provisions for both of you as you make your ascent. What effect will this extra weight have on your climb to the top? It will slow you down and tire you out. You will make less progress than you otherwise might; you may not even get to where you're going. This sounds unfair and impractical, doesn't it?

Surprisingly, this is what many women do on their life journeys. They let themselves become caretakers and carry their partners' emotional loads. Let your partner carry his or her own pack. You will lighten your load and your spirit.

Trail Warning #15: Being a Damsel in Distress

While there are some benefits to being the damsel in distress, such as a burly woodcutter in flannel coming to your rescue, there are some definite drawbacks. For example, you could be making your way through the forest and be eaten by a big bad wolf. Or you could realize that the woodcutter who came to rescue you is a con who just wants your basket of goodies. Without your basket of goodies, where would you be?

The problem these days is there's no such thing as a free rescue. You will be indebted to your rescuer for the rest of eternity. So rather than being a damsel in distress, be the indomitable damsel and learn to navigate your way through Sabotage Gulch. Along with your basket of goodies, pack a compass, mace, a survival kit, and a bad girl attitude.

Are you ready to stop the sabotage? Take the *Bad Girl Quiz* to find out. Read each question and then circle yes, no, or sometimes.

BAD GIRLS QUIZ

1. I use disclaimers.
   - a. Yes
   - b. No
   - c. Sometimes
2. I only apply for jobs if I have all the qualifications.
   - a. Yes
   - b. No
   - c. Sometimes
3. I regret not saying no to friends, family, or colleagues.
   - a. Yes
   - b. No
   - c. Sometimes
4. I'm polite to people who are inappropriate with me.
   - a. Yes
   - b. No
   - c. Sometimes
5. I worry about whether people like me or not.
   - a. Yes
   - b. No
   - c. Sometimes
6. If an employer, friend, or lover doesn't appreciate me, I speak up.
   - a. Yes
   - b. No
   - c. Sometimes
7. I am uncomfortable feeling like an imposter when pursuing my goals.
   - a. Yes
   - b. No
   - c. Sometimes
8. I carry my partner's emotional load.
   - a. Yes
   - b. No
   - c. Sometimes
9. I share my point of view whether or not I think people will agree with me.
   - a. Yes
   - b. No
   - c. Sometimes

10. Self-doubt makes it hard for me to take action.
    a. Yes   b. No   c. Sometimes
11. I refer to my body in everyday conversation.
    a. Yes   b. No   c. Sometimes

Answers:

1. a. 0 , b. 2, c. 1	7. a. 2, b. 0, c. 1
2. a. 2, b. 0, c. 1	8. a. 0, b. 2, c. 1
3. a. 0, b. 2, c. 1	9. a. 2, b. 0 c. 1
4. a. 0, b. 2, c. 1	10.a. 0, b. 2, c. 1
5. a. 2, b. 0, c. 1	11. a. 0, b. 2, c. 1
6. a. 0, b. 2, c. 1	

What was your score and what does it mean? Well, the bigger your score, the badder the bad girl. Find out where you fall in the bad girl scale.

Bad Girl Scale

22 Only!	Stiletto Girl
16–21	Platform Girl
11–15	Wedge Girl
6–10	Cuban Girl
0–5	Kitten Girl

Stop Sabotaging; Start Affirming

Rather than sabotaging yourself, practice building yourself up. Complete each of the following phrases.

I'm always the first to:

_____

_____

It was my idea to:

_____

_____

I'm amazed that I can:

_____

_____

Just this morning I:

_____

_____

Every day, I manage to:

_____

_____

Double Black Diamond Challenge

I am fed up with men who use sex like
a sleeping pill.
—Toni Braxton, pop singer

About This Trail: Double black diamond ski runs are insanely steep and populated with tricky bumps along the way. You'll have to embrace the bumps to get your finances in order and to get your groove on.

Duration: This trail takes forever if you don't have battery-operated sex toys and a trust fund. But seriously, you can't become a sexpert or a financial planner overnight. Money management and lovemaking are skills that will ripen with time, as long as you practice them on a regular basis.

Distance: If low self-esteem drives your purchases and choice of partners, your first step on this trail is to recognize you've got a problem. Then put one foot in front of the other . . .

Difficulty: Double black diamond ski runs are the steepest, but also the fastest. Take the challenge today and you'll soon speed ahead of the pack.

Backpack Essentials: While wearing red in the bedroom screams "ready for love," being in the red screams "dumb with money." Make sure to bring bank statements, pay stubs, and a calculator along with the *Kama Sutra* in paperback.

What to Leave Behind: Bounced checks, credit card debt, bad credit ratings, spending sprees, low libido, sexual hang-ups, and lousy lovers.

Early Pitfalls: Your fear of math. School kids can add, subtract, multiply, and divide, and so can you.

Trail Tip: Start early, because money doesn't grow on trees and love actually does cost something.

At the Trail's End: The lesson the Double Black Diamond Challenge will teach you is that great sex and healthy bank accounts don't just happen (for most of us). So it's important that bad girls get a leg up early in life, seeking out professional advice and taking steps to secure their footholds in both love and money matters.

What's the Double Black Diamond Challenge? Getting what you want in the bedroom and the boardroom. Sex and money are top priorities in a bonafide bad girl's life, and they are often cited as the primary problems in a couple's life. Yet American culture is very hush-hush about both topics. In this case, silence is not golden. It's been our experience that to get paid well, to have a healthy sex life, and to get your wish more often than not, you have to speak up and take action. It's not realistic to expect someone else to look out for your bank account or to read your lusty mind.

What can your lover (or you) do to make you moan, writhe, and squeal with delight? How much money should you stash away to make your life fabulous, fun, fulfilling, and financially sound? If you could see into the future, what would you want it to look like? When you look at your life today, what steps are you taking to get there?

The Stash

It's time to stash it away for a rainy day.

No matter how much money you or your household have or make, you'll never feel like you have enough. Even some millionaires fret that they're running out of money. Perceiving a lack of abundance is part of the human condition. Given your predictable psychological shortfall, you must start saving—even when you feel like you're on the brink of bankruptcy, living on the edge, falling into the moneyless abyss. Whether you're twenty-two or seventy-two, you *must* start saving today. Feeling like you don't have enough isn't a reason to put off saving. Feelings are fleeting. Money is a concrete necessity.

You may wonder where to start. We'll use an example from Ann's life to illustrate this point. Ann is reluctant to admit that she spends almost $4 a day at an unnamed coffee joint to get her designer coffee fix. It doesn't seem like much, but check this out: $4 x 30 days = $120. $120 x 12 months = $1,440. This is where you really need to pay attention: $1,440 x 20 years = $28,800. What a great start on a down payment for a summer home—for some java exec. Why is Ann paying for some java pusher's beachside cabana when she could have one of her own—umbrella drinks and all?

You may not be a java junkie, but you probably have other spending habits that seem inconsequential on a daily basis. It's time to do the math and start designing a better life for yourself.

Create a budget and stick to it.

So where should your paycheck go? In Boulder, we joke about food shopping at "Whole Paycheck" (Whole Foods), but how much you spend on food, shelter, and other necessities is serious business. As we get older and our responsibilities grow, so will our bills. Wake up, women of America—we ain't got no safety net! Unlike our neighbors to the North or across the pond, our paychecks have to cover health care (at the very least copays and deductibles), child care, maternity leave, and long-term care, and Social Security is quickly becoming Social Insecurity.

The first step to creating a budget is determining your fixed costs—things like rent, insurance, and loan payments. Anything you can do to keep down these costs will go a long way toward balancing your budget. Carol's first budget was based on a meager English teacher's salary. Apart from rent, her fixed costs were a monthly student loan payment, five dance classes a week, and a subway pass for transportation. Sticking to her budget, she managed to pay down her debt, invest in her dreams, and had some left over for midnight movies in Harvard Square and the occasional splurge on Indian food.

How'd she do it? First off, buying a car was never a consideration. A car payment and insurance would have wiped out her dance classes. She followed the 25 percent rule: housing costs should not exceed one-fourth of take-home pay. (This is a critical rule to stick to if you're renting.) Instead of living in the heart of Boston (forget making the student loan payments), she lived on the outskirts of downtown, but near a subway line. She also eschewed credit cards, knowing that they'd only get her into debt. Twenty years later, Carol still lives a pretty bohemian existence, but she's managed to pay off her student loans, start a retirement fund, and buy a sweet place in Boulder, Colorado. And she's still dancing. What's the lesson here? The spending habits you have today will determine your standard of living tomorrow.

Pace yourself.

Where does all your money go? To your mortgage or mocha lattes? To your hairstylist or your fund manager? To J Crew or JD Edwards? To T-Mobile or

T-bills? Into your gas tank or into a savings account? Money experts coach us to save, pay off debt, invest, and plan for retirement. Can you honestly say that you're doing all these things? By thirty or so, you should have choices: to buy your own place, go back to school, start a family, change your career path, or take time out for you. If you're approaching thirty, or just past it, pace yourself. Spending money as fast as you earn it will leave you with few options.

Pampering comes with a price tag.

A working girl deserves pampering, so there's nothing wrong with treating yourself to a spa retreat, indulging your senses in aromatic, edible treatments like a chocolate raspberry body scrub ($85), a pumpkin enzyme exfoliation ($100), a tingling mint foot mask ($55), or a lavender vanilla aromatherapy massage ($90). But keep a balance sheet of your splurges. They could easily add up to one or two full days off from work a year, which is the best pampering of all.

Don't turn into a pumpkin at midnight.

If you spend all your money getting ready for the ball, you'll end up in rags. How many of us indulge the inner diva and splurge for special events? What do you have to show for this? A closet full of Cinderella swag you can't even pawn off on friends?

A sleek updo that comes undone by the end of the night, highlights that go dull in a month, and sparkling nails that are chipped by your first glass of champagne?

Check out this "the purchase" versus "the piggy bank" chart. We've added up the most common expenses for special events: a trip to a local salon and a shopping spree at a popular chain store. So what's the damage? Almost $600, and that's assuming you don't buy any jewelry or hire a makeup artist.

Stuffing Your Closet vs. Stuffing Your Piggy Bank

The Purchase	The Piggy Bank
Cut, style, and shampoo	$75
Mani-pedi combo	$60
Silk chiffon empire waist dress	$150
Strappy stilettos	$185
Silk party clutch	$52
Elegant crocheted evening wrap	$48
Total:	$570

Wise up! You could spend way less and still incite envy and illicit lusty looks. Men don't spend nearly as much on this stuff and some of them look pretty darn good. The $600 is your rent or a mortgage payment.

It's a plane ticket to London and then some. Instead of throwing away money on fairy dust, you could be stuffing your piggy bank with cold, hard cash. So the next time a special event comes along, dig through your closets for hidden treasures before you head to the closest mall. If you haven't mastered the art of the classic upsweep or French manicures, put a call out to your bad girl girlfriends. And remember, piggy banks aren't just for kids.

Never pay full price when you could get a season's pass.

Carol and Ann are devoted fashionistas and admitted clothes hogs, but they don't go into debt for their stilettos or strappy tank tops. And although they pride themselves on being stylish, they boycott (or girlcott?) stores that charge $60 or more for clingy tops and bottoms whose primary purpose is soaking up sweat. What's their secret? They never, ever pay full price, and neither should you. There are always sales, especially online, and great deals at funky secondhand stores, and fancy discount ones like Tarzhay. And don't forget trades. You could host a clothes trading party with a group of girlfriends and find some new fashion treasures for free!

Let the professionals do the heavy lifting.

If you find yourself tiring of our math problems, why not let a professional do the heavy lifting? Make an investment (don't think of it as an expense) in financial software to create a budget and track your expenses. Then give your bank a call. Take advantage of services that can help you manage your budget. At the very least, you should sign up for direct deposit with your employer, set up automatic withdrawals for loan payments, and check into paying your bills online. Your bank may also offer attractive interest rates for certificates of deposit (CDs), which will earn you more interest than a savings account. And don't forget your retirement account: a Roth IRA is a girl's best friend.

Women's work doesn't pay.

While any entrepreneur will tell you that you've got to spend money to make it, you also have to make decent money to have some to spend. The problem many women face is their jobs just don't pay enough. Not sure what we mean? Let's compare the compensation for a few typical jobs for women and men:

- Police officers versus kindergarten teachers. While both professions serve the public good, serving and protecting is better compensated than serving and teaching.

- Nurses versus UPS drivers. The money's in taking packages, not pulses—if you work for UPS, that is. After thirty months, a UPS driver can earn up to $70,000 a year (Gary Strauss, USA Today, October 14, 2003).
- Tech support versus legal secretaries. Troubleshooting for an organization's network is far better remunerated than mastering the technicalities of the legal system.
- Housekeepers versus janitors. Being Mom's helper may earn you the title of "lifesaver," but a guy who probably spends most of his day in the janitor's closet makes more money than you do.
- Soccer moms versus chauffeurs. Okay, that one's not fair, but at least chauffeurs get paid for schlepping everyone around. According to Salary.com, the median expected salary for a senior-level chauffeur is over $45,000 a year.
- Preschool directors versus plumbers. You'll make more laying pipes than getting rambunctious toddlers to pipe down.

Here are the national estimates of the actual mean wages of these jobs:

Girl vs. Guy	The Job	The Pay
Girl	Kindergarten Teacher	$45,250
Guy	**Police Officer**	**$47,270**
Girl	Registered Nurse	$56,880
Guy	**UPS Driver**	**$70,000**
Girl	Legal Secretary	$39,070
Guy	**Technical Support**	**$53,750**
Girl	Housekeeper	$16,900
Guy	**Janitor**	**$18,790**
Girl	Preschool Director	$42, 270
Guy	**Plumber**	**$44,850**

Statistics from the US Dept. of Labor Bureau of Labor Statistics May 2005 Survey.

So what's a woman to do? Consider the paycheck you'll get if you do "women's work." Can you live with it? Are there comparable jobs that would pay you more? For example, if you're good with people, you'd make more in sales than services. If you're good with numbers, a CPA makes significantly more than a bookkeeper. And if teaching is your passion, public schools generally pay more than private ones, and education consultants make way more than teachers.

Carol grappled with the girl versus guy wage dilemma early in life. At age twelve she started making money doing what lots of girls do: baby-sitting.

And she was happy doing this. She made a buck an hour and her bank account was nearing four figures. What could be better than this? Snowblowing.

Just about the time Carol was starting out in her baby-sitting career, Boston was having its worst winter ever and her brother Kenny was raking it in. After a full day of snowblowing neighbors' driveways, Kenny had a wad of cash that could barely fit in his front jeans pocket. After a full day of baby-sitting, Carol could slip the money she made into her training bra.

What did Carol do about this inequity? She did the practical thing: she cut back on the baby-sitting during the blizzard months and joined forces with her brother. Playing second fiddle to a big-time snowblower was better than playing Barbies for a buck an hour.

Demand a fair wage.

That's just what Carol did when she realized she was getting screwed in the salary department in her first job out of college. She was doing women's work— teaching—and she loved it. But it didn't make sense to her that she was paid so little. "Wait a minute," Carol challenged. "This is a multinational corporation—they've got schools all over the world and customers are paying beaucoup bucks for these classes, and they can't afford to give us health insurance? I'm cranking out six hours a day of teaching for them, going to unpaid meetings during my lunch hour, and *they can't cough up health insurance?"*

She asked the director of the school if there was a remedy for this situation. The director's reply was, "Sorry, there is no such thing as national health insurance, so we just can't offer that." When Carol rebutted "Yes, there is. There's BlueCross BlueShield," the director limply responded, "I'm not familiar with that."

Realizing she was getting nowhere, Carol wrote a letter to corporate headquarters, had all the teachers sign it, and requested a reply within thirty days. One month later, everyone got a $1,000 a year raise, and one year later, everyone got health insurance from BlueCross BlueShield. Not bad for one letter, huh?

Statistics That'll Scare You into Saving Today

Think you can put off saving for your love nest, dream home, or nest egg? Think again. Here are some statistics to help you stop spending and start saving today.

Older women:
- The United States has the highest poverty rate of older women of all postindustrial nations.

One out of every four women over sixty-five lives below the federal poverty line (Seniors Site, http://www.seniors-site.com).

Single women:
- Single women comprise 40 percent of all bankruptcy filings (M. P. Dunleavey, columnist, "7 Ways to Fight off Bankruptcy," MSN Money).

Divorced women:
- A person who marries and stays married accumulates nearly twice as much personal wealth as a person who is single or divorced. Those who divorce lose, on average, 75 percent of their personal net worth (Jay Zagorsky, research scientist at Ohio State University's Center for Human Resource Research, http://www.chrr.ohio-state.edu).

Working women:
- Two out of three working women earn less than $30,000 a year, and nine out of ten earn less than $50, 000 (Women's Institute for a Secure Retirement, http://www.wiser.heinz.org).

Stay-at-home moms:
- Economists estimate that women who give up careers to stay home may lose up to $1 million over the years (M. P. Dunleavey, columnist,

"Cost of Being a Stay-at-Home Mom: $1 Million," MSN Money).

- A woman who takes two years off from work loses an average of 18 percent of her income on returning. If she's out three years or more, she may lose up to 38 percent (Sylvia Ann Hewlett and Carolyn Buck Luce, Center for Work-Life Policy, http://www.worklifepolicy.org).

Women with high school degrees:
- Men with high school educations earned a median income of $31,477 in 1998, while the median income of women high school graduates was $22,780 (American Association of University Women, http://www.aauw.org).

Women with college degrees:
- A typical twenty-five-year-old woman with a college degree will earn at least $500,000 less than a college-educated man over a lifetime (Women's Institute for a Secure Retirement, http://www.wiser.heinz.org).

Everything's negotiable.

You should know that when you start a new job, everything's negotiable. So negotiate. If you're given a salary range that just is not what you expect and is not the going market rate, ask for more. Remember, your starting salary will determine how much you earn in the future, too. If your employer "saved" on you with a lowball offer, it'll be hard to make this up with future raises.

Carol learned this the hard way. She accepted a promotion that was presented as a done deal, "Yeah, payroll has already been notified." A few weeks later she found out that one of the low performers she had to supervise, a guy, was making more money than she was.

Act entitled.

Employers have learned that they can push us harder and pay us less. While our male counterparts sail through life doing less and demanding more, we work harder and then fret that we don't know enough. How do you explain this? A sense of entitlement. Most men possess one; most women do not. We've got to change that. If you do not feel genuinely entitled to a better job, higher pay, or more respect, act like you do. Confront your discomfort with this strange new feeling called entitlement, and you'll finally get what you deserve.

You don't need a man to pitch a tent.

SATC (Sex and the City) fans will remember Carrie's shock when she realizes she's spent the equivalent of a down payment ($40,000) on her Jimmy Choos and Manolo Blahniks, while her more budget-conscious friends Miranda and Samantha were already Manhattan home owners. Luckily, more and more single women are taking after Carrie's friends. In the United States and Europe, they are outpacing single men in real estate purchases by a margin of 56 percent to 47 percent, according to the National Association of Realtors. Over the past few years, interest among women in home-improvement courses and tools has also grown. So don't buy into the myth: first comes love, then comes real estate. Your dream home is just a down payment away.

Team up to buy supplies.

You don't have to be good at math to know that two can live more cheaply than one. So if you're single, it's time to double up. Diversify your options and increase your purchasing power by seeking out savvy and supportive partnerships with friends and family. Leverage the relationships that you have nurtured; let these relationships nurture you. For example, if you can't afford to buy a place on your own, there may be a family member, friend, or acquaintance that is looking for a real estate investment and will invest with you. If you already own a place, why not offset your monthly mortgage and utility bills by renting out a room—long or short term? If you live in a tourist-friendly area, renting out your place on weekends or a week at a time is easier than you think thanks to craigslist. And don't forget to buy in bulk. You don't have to be a family of five to shop and save at discount stores. Team up with your loved ones to buy food and other essentials and be a winner in the singles game.

Women can hunt and gather, too.

An obvious statement, we know, but most of us were brought up with the notion that our future husbands should make more money than us—and if necessary, they should be able to support us. What's wrong with this thinking? It's sexist!

What about when you have kids, you ask. Well, you know, maybe you won't have kids. Or maybe you'll be bringing in so much cash, you'll want Dad to stay at home. Or maybe, just maybe, when all the planets align and the world is a perfect place, women won't have to choose work over family or family over work (this is our sincere hope).

Sex

Learn the ropes.

When Carol was six years old, she received a creative but not entirely accurate explanation of where babies come from. At this tender age, Carol became very curious about the topic. She knew her mother played a major role in putting her on the planet, but she was sure her father was just some guy who lived with her family. When she asked her mother where she came from, the answer was, "Your father and I went to church and prayed for you." "And?" said Carol. "And you started growing in my belly and you came out nine months later," said her mother. That sounded pretty believable to Carol. "So Dad didn't have anything to do with it, did he?" said Carol feeling vindicated. "Yes, he did," answered her mom. "He prayed." Carol's friends eventually filled her in on the missing pieces, but it was years later. What's the moral of this story? Don't wait until you're all grown up to get the facts—become a sexpert now.

Don Juan versus the Ho

Time keeps moving forward, but society's view of sexually liberated women is stuck in reverse. Girls who have casual sex are labeled ho or slut, but the guys they sleep with earn fun titles like player. How can we change this? We've got to come up with new labels—good ones! Right now, we're stuck with degrading tags such as whore, floozy, femme fatale, hooker, vamp, skank, slut, prostitute, wench, vixen, bimbo, bitch, naughty, nasty, nympho, loose, tart, tramp, and hussy. On the other hand, our partners in crime enjoy titles such as player, stud, stallion, ladykiller, bad boy, Don Juan, Romeo, and Casanova. Why are there so many negative names for sexually active women and so few for men? Let's use some positive ones, shall we? Sex goddess, mankiller, hot mama, saucy sister, fine feline, Aphrodite, juicy Julia, steamy Shakti, tantric Tamara, and erotic Eve.

The next time you get together with your girlfriends, come up with your own verbiage for a woman with sexual prowess. Send them in. We'd love to post them and start a buzz.

Read the ultimate guide: *Cosmo.*

First stop in your sexpert development? *Cosmo.* Orgasms Unlimited, Sexercises, and the Kama Sutra Match and Moan game are just a few of the lust lessons and love techniques regularly featured in *Cosmopolitan* magazine. Thanks to Helen Gurley Brown, *Cosmo* has been selling sex for sex's sake for over forty years now, raising women's expectations in the pleasure department, the bedroom, and most other rooms in the house. While *Cosmo* may not be as detailed as the *Kama Sutra*, its R&D department has developed a spicy alternative called the Kama

Sutra Match and Moan game. Participants try out sex positions of varying degrees of difficulty, and then rate them on the moan meter. We were especially delighted with the side slide (you won't find this one at your local water park), the thigh master (now we understand why Suzanne Somers is sexy at sixty), the randy rider (you don't have to be a cowgirl to master it), and the tilt-a-girl (a thrilling ride from the first thrust forward). After playing a quick game or two of Moan and Match, we demand a rematch. (More! More! More!)

Get professional instruction.

If getting adventurous in the bedroom leads to bodily injury or a 911 call, you need professional instruction. After all, batting an eyelash should heat up your relationship, not require an emergency rescue from the local fire department. Fortunately for us, Boulder is a hot bed—literally—of workshops, retreats, and coaching in sacred sex, sexual healing, and intimacy coaching. Find out what's available in your area. Sexual healing may be just a Google search away.

Reach your peak.

Orgasms are not only "oh, so good" but they're also good for you. Orgasms tone your pelvic muscles and release endorphins. They also relieve tension and help you sleep. The health benefits are so compelling that we recommend you include them in your daily recommended allowances. So try slipping them in with your morning coffee, afternoon tea, or midnight snack. And if you don't have a partner, we suggest you make some new friends. We'd like to introduce you to Jack Rabbit, Mr. Bendy, and the Rock Chick, who live in a local superstore or sextoy website near you.

Don't hook up with a guy who won't hit the trail with you.

Although you can tell a bad girl a mile away, guys who are bad for you are harder to spot. How can you be sure your guy can handle a bad girl? Read the signs:

Top Ten Signs He's Not into Bad Girls

10. He falls for women who are one meal away from anorexia.
9. He likes that you make money, as long as he makes *more* money.
8. He's the expert, which is why he's always right.
7. He thinks sexual harassment is a "scam."
6. He's the king and you're his handmaiden, which is why he expects you to wait on him hand and foot.

5. He likes to play follow the leader: he leads, you follow.

4. He's shocked and angered when you swear in front of his friends.

3. He thinks a dirty girl is someone who does his laundry.

2. He doesn't believe in reciprocity. Just because you went down on him doesn't mean . . .

And the number one sign that he's not into bad girls is . . .

1. He says he's into bad girls. You know the old adage, If you have to say it, then . . .

It can be dangerous.

Adventurous sex can cause you to bang your head on the bedpost or fall off the kitchen table. But seriously folks, unsafe sex can give you more than a bump on the head. You don't have to be a teen to get genital herpes or AIDs. Your sexual partners may have VD, STDS, AIDS, and other acronyms. Know your partners (and ask them if they are infected with any of these). Don't let an acronym catch you unprotected. Use *latex* condoms.

It's about pleasure, not performance.

What words would you use to describe amazing sex? *Slow and sensuous? Tousled and entwined? Uncontainable and acrobatic? Spontaneous and forbidden? Hot, wet, and salty?* What words wouldn't you use? *Predictable? Perfectly planned? Photogenic?* Those of you who videotape have found out that last one's generally not true. The point is that sex is about pleasure, not performance. It doesn't have to be a perfectly choreographed porn duet from start to finish—unless you're working in a live sex show in Amsterdam. If people are paying good money to see you bump and grind, by all means give them their money's worth. But for the non-professional, sex should be about pleasure. So if fresh air and hiking spark something between you and your partner, get dirty. Turn off the trail and fall into some bushes and make glorious, sweaty love in your hiking boots and gore-tex.

Ultimatums

What do ultimatums have to do with the Double Black Diamond Challenge? Ultimatums shift the balance of power. Ultimatums come in when you have spoken up but no one is listening. They shift the balance of power so that you are heard! And they let the person who's holding out on you—your boss, your partner, your boytoy—know that there are negative consequences for ignoring, disrespecting, or underappreciating you. Finally, ultimatums are not a bluff. You've got to deliver them like you mean them *and* follow through with your threats.

If you're an ultimatum virgin, you're either a fully realized bad girl that no one messes with or you're a chicken. For the chickens, we've provided some examples. We've also left space for you to craft ultimatums for your particular situations.

	Situation	Ultimatum
LOVE	Your man won't wear a condom.	Either you cover that in latex or you practice celibacy.
	Your long-time live-in lover doesn't want to get married, but you do.	Either we set a date today or you're moving out tomorrow.
WORK	Your boss tells you—yet again—that there's just not enough money in the budget for the raise you've been promised.	I'm sorry to hear that. Please accept my two-week notice.
	You're a contract employee, and your employer wants to cut your hourly pay—it's the budget excuse again.	You may as well cut me, because I don't work for less than $x an hour.
LOVE		
WORK		

BAD GIRL QUIZ

1. I put away money for major purchases (e.g., a car, a house, a home improvement, or things for the new baby).

    a. Yes   b. No   c. Sometimes

2. I choose jobs that have potential for professional development and significant salary increases over time.

    a. Yes   b. No   c. Sometimes

3. I don't set spending limits for clothes, salon visits, and so on for special events like weddings and parties.

    a. Yes   b. No   c. Sometimes

4. I engage in retail therapy when I'm bored, unhappy, or when I need an emotional boost.

    a. Yes   b. No   c. Sometimes

5. I seek out professional help (books, people, software) to improve my budgeting and financial planning skills.

    a. Yes   b. No   c. Sometimes

6. When I'm in the mood and my lover's not handy, I masturbate.

    a. Yes   b. No   c. Sometimes

7. I disapprove of women who sleep around.

     a. Yes   b. No   c. Sometimes

8. If an orgasm is something I want, I can give myself one or show my partner how.

     a. Yes   b. No   c. Sometimes

9. I ask sexual partners about their sexual history only after we've gotten to know each other.

     a. Yes   b. No   c. Sometimes

10. I feel inhibited having sex if I've gained a few pounds, or if I'm feeling fat.

     a. Yes   b. No   c. Sometimes

Answers:

1. a. 2, b. 0, c. 1	6. a. 2, b. 0, c. 1
2. a. 2, b. 0, c. 1	7. a. 0, b. 2, c. 1
3. a. 0, b. 2, c. 1	8. a. 2, b. 0, c. 1
4. a. 0, b. 2, c. 1	9. a. 0, b. 2, c. 1
5. a. 2, b. 0, c. 1	10. a. 0, b. 2, c. 1

What was your score and what does it mean? Well, the bigger your score, the badder the bad girl. Find out where you fall in the bad girl scale.

Bad Girl Scale

20 Only!	Stiletto Girl
15–19	Platform Girl
10–14	Wedge Girl
5–9	Cuban Girl
0–4	Kitten Girl

Sassy Comeback Arch

The thing women have yet to learn is nobody gives you power. You just take it.
—Roseanne Barr

About This Trail: Sassy Comeback Arch is an ascent that requires rock climbing. If you doubt your abilities or falter, you may find yourself taking a screamer (a long fall).

Duration: Once you are infused with the spirit of sassiness, you will move like Spider Woman to the apex of the arch.

Distance: If you discover the shortcut, you'll summit the arch in a snap. If you don't, you'll need a portaledge for sleeping (snoozing in a precariously hung hammock on a rock ledge).

Difficulty: It depends. If you're a Snow White or Cinderella type, this trail is grueling. If you're like Calamity Jane or Annie Oakley, this trail is a yawner.

Elevation: If you scale the arch, you'll be in bad girl heaven with your head in the clouds.

Backpack Essentials: Sassy sauce, guerrilla tactics, sassy comeback grab bag, peckers and pitons (for climbing protection), a quick tongue, and a firm grasp.

What to Leave Behind: Sugar and spice and everything nice.

Early Pitfalls: Beware the quicksand of self-doubt at the base of the arch; the deeper you sink into it, the harder it is to get out.

Trail Tip: Sassy comebacks are like pitons—the more you use them, the more powerful and secure you'll feel.

At the Trail's End: You will transform yourself into a calm, assertive woman who can deflect negative comments and defend herself against verbal attacks without breaking a sweat or losing a heel.

———————

The word *cairn* is Scottish in origin and means "a pile of rocks." Cairns are often used to mark hiking trails and it's traditional for each person passing by a cairn to add a stone to counteract the destructive effects of weather. Imagine that your personal power is equal to the size of a cairn. The bigger your cairn, the greater your power. To maintain your power, you'll need to keep your cairn stacked high; to increase it, you'll need to pile on more rocks.

So how do you do this? As you go about your day, be alert to situations in which someone is disrespectful, demeaning, intimidating, or just downright rude to you and then stand your ground and fight back. Are we saying that a bad girl's life must include daily brawls? Not at all, but it should involve the use of strategic tactics. We've devised one that is much better than throwing stones or hurling insults. We call it *the sassy comeback*.

Sassy comebacks are zingers, one-liners delivered in a calm, sassy manner. They are clever, powerful, and usually very funny lines that the greedy cairn robbers won't soon forget. They allow you to regain your rocks, and then pile them up as high as you want.

We invite you to dig through our pile of comebacks and see which ones you want to add your cairn. Then, start using them right away. The next time a Neanderthal stones you with a demeaning comment or behavior, lose the deer-in-the-headlights expression and hurl a sassy comeback. Having tossed aside the excess emotional baggage that comes from negative interactions and negative people, you'll soon be walking on air. Oh, how good it feels to be clever, and wicked, and sassy!

Ann will attest to the fact that preparing for the future with sassy comebacks works wonders. After working on this chapter, she felt as if years of good girl conditioning were washed right out of her hair and down the drain.

At Work

Men *and women* at work can be as unpredictable and savage in their behavior as wild animals. Awakened from their complacency by your sassy saunter, supreme self-confidence, and lightning fast pace on the trail, they lash out when they can't keep up with you. But you can tame them without using a chair or a whip or dulling the heel of your four-inch stilettos.

You wouldn't understand.

We've stolen a story from Carol's mother, Margo, for this one. She is the baddest of bad girls and we love her for it! Margo was at a meeting with other executives (she's number two in the company) and a finance guy was giving a presentation. As he reviewed the numbers, Margo asked for some clarification. Instead of being a professional and giving her the information she had asked for, he said, "You wouldn't understand." Boy did he regret that!

Margo's sassy comeback: "Do I have to grow a penis to understand this?"

You're not the right person for this.

Your boss tells you that you're not the right person to give an important presentation. He doesn't think the audience (top executives) will find you credible. After all, you do look awfully young and you're so approachable and friendly. He thinks that Bob, a man who is less experienced and couldn't give a presentation to save his life, is the "man" for the job.

Sassy comeback: Sure I am. The man for this job is a woman. And that woman is me.

Are you sure?

Wow! We can't tell you how many times men—only men—have asked us this question. For some reason, only men have doubted our abilities to do what we're very, very qualified to do.

Sassy comeback: No, of course not. Everything I say and do I just pull out of my ass.

You can't talk to me like that.

Most men and lots of women don't believe women have any business being authority figures. If we're the teachers, the managers, the parents, or the bosses, we are the authority figures and we can and will tell you what to do.

Sassy comeback: I just did.

Can you do this? You're so much better at it or I just don't know how to . . .

Beware the helpless man who is capable of running a global company or a regional division but doesn't know how to run a dishwasher or a vacuum. This same man can navigate international travel and client sites, but can't figure out how to navigate through the supermarket to get his family's groceries for the week. If this man asks you to do something for him because "you're so much better at it," he's trying to get out of "lowly girl work," things like taking notes during a meeting, writing cards to friends and family, taking care of the kids, and cleaning the house. Simply remind this man of the old adage . . .

Sassy comeback: Practice makes perfect.

You should . . .

The should guy. You've met a few, haven't you? They're the ones who say, "That's not how you do it. You're doing it all wrong. Let me show you . . ." Some men just can't resist showing a woman what to do. We suppose they think that when they're not around, we're completely paralyzed with helplessness. Don't waste your time on them. Know when the best thing to say is . . .

Sassy comeback: Apparently, you don't know who I am.

I respect women.

Beware the man who feels the need to say this. He's definitely got "issues" with women; otherwise, why would he say it? You know the expression, If he has to say it . . . One guy who said this was a boss, a director of a department in a high-tech company. Women were leaving his department left and right, fed up with the boys' club he'd created. The only respect that he regularly enforced was respect for his authority. His female employees should have called him on his hypocrisy by saying . . .

Sassy comeback: Sure could have fooled me.

You're too aggressive/assertive/pushy for a woman.

We may have entered a new millennium, but there are still people living in the dark ages. (Think caves, monosyllabic language, basket weaving, berry picking, and woolly mammoth hunts.) These primitive people are offended by assertive behavior because they think women will display their hunting prowess and show that they're fully capable of bringing down the woolly mammoth. And where would that leave Neanderthal men? Berry picking in loin cloths?

These cave-dwellers think aggression is reserved for males. After all, it wouldn't be very ladylike to speak your mind, grab the spotlight, push someone out of your way, demand attention, or give someone a piece of your mind.

Sassy comeback: Then I guess you'd better get out of my way.

You need to be perkier or more bubbly.

Women workers can be driving semis, using jackhammers, drilling for oil, slinging pancakes, shoveling manure, or fishing for salmon and they are sometimes still expected to be perky. Granted, there are some jobs that require perkiness—including cheerleading, competing in beauty pageants, baton twirling, clowning, and reality TV show hosting, but in most cases, perkiness is *not* a job requirement. For some reason, a number of male bosses demand this of their female underlings, especially the ones that were geeks in high school. It's as if every male has to have his perky female quotient and these guys are making up for lost time.

Ann did a stint as a program manager for an international education organization. One day she learned that the president was unhappy with her performance. When she later asked him what the problem was, he, being an exacting Ivy Leaguer, chose his words carefully.

He said, "We need program specialists who are bubbly." Then, restating his comment so that it was more concise, he said, "We need bubbles for program managers."

Bubbles? As in round-floating-in-air-about-to-pop bubbles? At the time, Ann was stunned and tongue-tied. But if she had it to do over, she would have handled it differently.

Sassy comeback: Do you really want me to be a transparent, vacant, popping substance?

(For Ann's full story on perkiness and bubbles, see the Epilogue.)

At Play (in the Street)

Skipping along a creekside path on the way to your next adventure, you round a corner and bam, there's a fellow human being—a friend even—poised to pounce on you. How do you avert danger while staying on the trail? Our advice: Don't tread lightly. People who try to take the bounce out of your step need to be stopped in their tracks. A sassy comeback will allow you to stand your ground and then gracefully continue on your way.

You're not very sexual, are you?

A friend of Carol's said this to her. Needless to say, he isn't her friend anymore. Men who tell you that you aren't sexual or sexual enough want you to deliver the goods. They say they're okay with being your friend, but they're not and they resent it. How dare you deny them what they want!

Sassy comeback: Sure I am. I'm just not attracted to you.

You're a tease. (Read: you're giving me the signal you want sex.)

When men are accused of teasing it means they're joking around or enjoying some innocent flirting. When a woman's a tease, it means she's holding out, turning a guy on without putting out, or not being very "nice." How did being nice come to mean having sex with every guy you flirt with or are friendly to? Girls, you'd better not give in to this line—give 'em a sassy comeback instead.

Ann had a male coworker, Jason, who was married with four kids. During the workday they would joke around and play practical jokes on people. On the last day of the project, he offered to walk her out to her car. Thinking nothing of it, she agreed. As a going-away present, he grabbed her hand and stuck it on top of his happy package to share the wealth. She recoiled in horror, saying he had the wrong idea. He then accused her of flirting and leading him on. As proof he said, "You laughed at my jokes." Ann wondered why laughing at jokes meant foreplay?

Sassy comeback: And that's my problem because. . . Oh, it's not my problem. (Note: This sassy comeback has multiple applications.)

You're not very nice.

Women who are sassy might experience some backlash, especially from men. Some men will tell you you're mean, you don't act like women they know, or gosh darn it, you just aren't very nice. We think that being nice is like vanilla ice cream: it's boring and tasteless. If you're being labeled "nice," you should consider a change in behavior—be a bitch on wheels or at least cynical or disinterested every now and then. Remember, when we use the term "nice girl" to describe a woman it usually means she's virginal, subdued, ladylike—boring! So if someone tells you that you aren't nice, take it as a compliment.

Sassy comeback: I'll be nicer if you agree to be more interesting.

You look like a little girl!

Uh, oh! Watch out for a man who says this—he's got a serious schoolgirl fetish. He's fantasizing about you in a pinafore dress and knee socks. The man who said this was a college professor, married with two kids. Carol was teaching his kids English. One day he tricked her into a lunch date, telling her it was a farewell lunch with his family who would soon return to Korea. He showed up alone. And then after lunch, he grabbed her butt as a friendly good-bye. How did Carol put a stop to his transgressions? She said . . .

Sassy comeback: Actually, I'm a grown woman who is going to tell your wife what you've been up to.

C'mon, how about a smile for me?

How many times have you been asked to deliver a smile for a guy's viewing pleasure? You could be trudging through ankle-deep snow and slush with a bag full of groceries and a migraine and some strange dude asks you for "a little smile." You could be balancing a full tray of drinks over your head while navigating through a crowded bar and a man says, "C'mon, babe, how 'bout a smile." (When Ann was mugged, her mugger asked her for a smile. Needless to say, her face muscles were frozen in terror.) She wishes she would have said, "You can either have money or a smile, but you can't have both."

Sassy comeback: I smile only for people I like.

You are so tall/fat/large—anything other than slender and petite.

Why is it that a woman's body shape, height, and weight are up for public display and comment? If a woman is anything other than the perfect ideal, people, especially men, feel compelled to comment. I mean, do we feel the need to draw attention to bald men who could use a rug, dudes with breasts who could use a manzere, or short guys who could use a pair of stilts?

How should you deal with body commentary? We borrowed a sassy comeback from a friend of Carol's. Lena, a 5-foot, 11-inch woman, was living in Japan for a few years. Japanese men would constantly comment on her height. "You are so tall!" they would proclaim. After several such incidents, she grew tired of the height commentary. The next time a man felt compelled to point out her height, she responded with, "And you are so small." This quickly put an end to inane remarks she encountered and sent any guy who dared comment, cowering. Lena could stroll down the streets of Tokyo in peace, towering above the men and loving it.

Sassy comeback: And you've got a tiny vocabulary.

I didn't gain an ounce when I was pregnant—except what the baby weighed.

Guess I was lucky.

You stare in disbelief at the stick figure with an infant, who's looking you up and down. She's practicing classic one-up behavior, telling you in no uncertain terms that women like her, ones who stay rail thin when pregnant, are superior to ones who don't. She's indicating that she doesn't see you as a luminous healthy pregnant woman, but as a failure for putting on "baby weight."

Sassy comeback: Guess your baby was lucky, too—that she actually came out healthy.

A man touches you inappropriately on a train/plane/bus/city street.

For some reason, a handful of men think they're at a petting zoo when they encounter attractive women in public places. They reach out and touch, grab, pinch, and rub up against us. If this happens to you, we have several sassy comebacks in our arsenal to warn men that you're in fact a poisonous snake with fangs and venom. They can pet at their own risk.

If a guy rubs up against you on a crowded train, it's time to use your stilettos. (You knew they'd come in handy.) Other heels will also suffice. This move requires nonchalance and fancy footwork. Step back hard on the intruder's foot and dig your stiletto heel into his toes while not even looking up from your reading material. The bumping and grinding dude will do the pinched toe cha-cha-cha and quickly chasse to the other side of the train.

If a guy grabs you, simply reach out and snag his hand and say very loudly . . .

Sassy comeback: Whose hand is this?

Sassy Comeback Grab Bag

We've asked our friends for some of their favorite sassy comebacks and we've added them to our sassy comeback grab bag. You can mix and match these comebacks for a grab bag full of sassiness. Tote them with you wherever you go; you never know when you'll need them.

Situation or Comment	Sassy Comeback
Someone makes an unreasonable request of you	"How does never work for you?"

"You're difficult/high maintenance."	"I'm easy to get along with once you learn to worship me."
"Why aren't you married yet?"	"I have enough laundry, thank you."
"Why don't you have any children?"	"I was hoping to do something meaningful with my life."
A guy does something offensive	"I should report you, but you're not worth it."
Any form of mild harassment at work or play	"Does that complete the harassment portion of the program?"
Guys making catcalls, leering, or otherwise acting like wild animals	"Who let you out of the zoo?"
Any rude comment from a man	"Would you say that to your daughter or sister?"
"You're a bitch."	"You say bitch like it's a bad thing."
Strange, erratic, or annoying behavior	"Isn't it time for your medication?"
A person shares an unwanted opinion	"When I want your point of view, I'll give it to you" or "I don't remember asking for you opinion."
A person talks to you in a condescending tone	"And your point is?"
An annoying guy won't leave you alone	"I'm trying to imagine you with a personality."

A man is being arrogant and egotistical	"Is your ego making up for your penis?"
"Are you PMSing?"	"Yes, my progesterone level is dangerously low and I have a gun."
A guy who's being a jerk has the nerve to ask you for your phone number	"Sure. It's 1-800-Goodluck-withthat."
A dude at work is ordering you around	"Yeah, sure. I'll get right on it."
You're being pursued by an unwanted suitor and want to put a stop to it	"I don't think we're a good match. You're a healthy heterosexual man, and I'm a bisexual hermaphrodite."
A muscle-bound guy comes out of the surf with a handful of shells (mussels). He shows them to you and says, "Wanna see some muscles?"	"Sure, where are they?"
Your boss who pushes (mostly female) employees to overextend themselves is trying to add something to your plate	"I really wish I could do it, but it would take my focus away from my current project."
A guy on a plane volunteers you to move to the middle seat—because you're smaller than the guy who's in it	"This is the seat I paid for, so this is the seat I'm sitting in."
A neighborhood mom suggests you "team up" for babysitting duties. She's got three kids, you've got one.	"I'd love to help out, but I'm booked solid. Try me again in a year."

Write Your Own Sassy Comebacks

What's your sassy comeback scenario? What comments make you burn because they're meant to put you down or keep you in your place? Don't you just wish you were prepared with a sassy comeback for these occasions? Write your comebacks. Get sassy!

1. He or she says:

_____

_____

_____

Your sassy comeback:

_____

_____

_____

2. He or she says:

_____

_____

_____

Your sassy comeback:

_____

_____

_____

BAD GIRL QUIZ

1. When someone makes an inappropriate comment, I usually ignore it.
   - a. Yes
   - b. No
   - c. Sometimes
2. When a colleague puts me down at work, I get depressed.
   - a. Yes
   - b. No
   - c. Sometimes
3. I feel empowered when I set verbal limits.
   - a. Yes
   - b. No
   - c. Sometimes
4. I hope people are attuned enough to know what I want so I don't have to spell it out for them.
   - a. Yes
   - b. No
   - c. Sometimes
5. I think sassy comebacks are disrespectful.
   - a. Yes
   - b. No
   - c. Sometimes
6. It feels good to reply to inappropriate comments with zingers.
   - a. Yes
   - b. No
   - c. Sometimes
7. When someone has insulted me, I stew about it for days.
   - a. Yes
   - b. No
   - c. Sometimes
8. I usually take the path of least resistance and avoid conflict.
   - a. Yes
   - b. No
   - c. Sometimes

9. I believe that I don't have to tolerate catcalls, whistling, and harassment by men.

      a. Yes   b. No   c. Sometimes

10. I believe that sassiness can be cultivated.

      a. Yes   b. No   c. Sometimes

Answers:

1. a. 0 , b. 2, c. 1   6. a. 2, b. 0, c. 1
2. a. 0, b. 2, c.1   7. a. 0, b. 2, c. 1
3. a. 2, b. 0, c. 1   8. a. 0, b. 2, c. 1
4. a. 0, b. 1, c. 2   9. a. 2, b. 0, c. 1
5. a. 0, b. 2, c. 1   10. a. 2, b. 0, c. 1

What was your score and what does it mean? Well, the bigger your score, the more sassy you are. Find out where you fall in the bad girl scale.

Bad Girl Scale

20 Only!	Stiletto Girl
15–19	Platform Girl
10–14	Wedge Girl
5–9	Cuban Girl
0–4	Kitten Girl

Bushwhackers' Gorge

It's risky, but then a lot of people die out there driving. Still, I get into my car.
—Chris Bockoff

About This Trail: This gorge is for trailblazers. That's who these women are and that's the only way to get to the summit. Did you really think there'd be an easier way?

Duration: The more you seek out the wisdom of bad girl mentors, the faster you'll finish this climb. (Think of mentors as escalators—they'll whiz you to the top!)

Distance: Most women do not complete this trail in their lifetimes. Be the exception.

Difficulty: Afraid of heights? Find your courage. More than a few of our interviewees advise budding bad girls that the first step to finding their path is to find their courage.

Elevation: This trail doesn't end at 10,000, 14,000, or even 28,000 feet. These women summit physical and personal mountains over and over again.

Backpack Essentials: A 'tude, tenaciousness, raw talent, timely treats, a few tricks up your sleeve, and a turban. (Okay, maybe not a turban, unless it's in this season's collection.)

What to Leave Behind: Fear. What's to fear? You lived through monsters under your bed and in the closet. You'll live through this, too.

Early Pitfalls: When the trail gets tough, there's always the temptation to turn around. So keep telling yourself: there's chocolate at the top, and a gift bag overflowing with aromatic spa products, really! Oh, yeah, and you'll get a free massage.

Trail Tip: It'll be easier to summit if you're following the lead of a bad girl. Fasten your rope to hers and let her guide you to the top.

At the Trail's End: You'll learn that even the most talented, courageous, intelligent, and hardworking bad girls face obstacles on the trail. They may have stumbled and fallen a few times, but they always pick themselves up and keep on trekking. And so should you.

Though they differ widely in age, attitude, aptitude, personal choices, and personality, each one of these women has blazed a unique and adventurous trail. Bushwhacking in the bad girl backcountry, they've created extreme possibilities for themselves and other risk takers. And now that they have carved out a swath of arduous yet accessible trails, they're throwing down a rope to help the rest of us get there, too.

The American Dream: Margo Brunelli

(Age seventy-three, vice president of operations, mother of five, and grandmother of five)

At age seventeen, Mairead Greene left her tiny Irish village and ten siblings to chase her girlhood dream of becoming a midwife and having her own car and house. She made a beeline for the bright lights and the big city to study nursing and midwifery in London. Sixty hours a week of cleaning bedpans, doling out prescription drugs, and studying nights got her a nursing degree and a midwifery certification seven years later. Traveling by bicycle, she delivered over three hundred babies as a country midwife in Ireland. She eventually ditched the bike for a cross-Atlantic ride in a 727, landing in Boston, Massachusetts, in 1960. Today Margo is approaching her golden wedding anniversary and has five college-educated kids and five boisterous grandchildren. She's climbed her way to the top in the corporate world, landing herself the job of executive VP of operations at a health care company at the age of fifty-six.

How does our definition of bad girl apply to you?

I've always spoken out and told the truth. Some people might consider that breaking the rules, but I don't. There's nothing impolite about speaking your piece. You have an obligation to yourself.

I also don't believe in following rules that don't make any sense. I was raised to believe that sex before marriage was a sin and that sex in marriage was only for having children. When I became pregnant with my fifth child, I decided it was time to talk to the parish priest. During confession, I told him that as soon as I had the baby, I was going to practice birth control. His response was, it's not a sin until you do it. Well, I did it. And I have never gone back to the confessional.

Putting men in their place is a theme for Margo.

One day at work I had had yet another disagreement with a guy (appropriately named "Dick") and he suggested we meet with the owner of the company to discuss it. I agreed to this not only to resolve the conflict, but also to test the owner. Was he sincere about supporting me? Did he really appreciate what I was doing for him?

At the meeting, I explained that I was insulted by Dick's behavior toward me. The owner immediately lit into him. "Cut the shit, Dick," he said. "Margo's built this company." Dick never gave me any problems after that.

We asked Margo about how she's achieved as much as she has.

I came from a big family, number eight of a litter of eleven. I had to believe in myself just to survive. I went out into the world confident. When times are tough, I think, "I'll survive this."

Do you think being a woman has presented you with unique challenges?

Definitely. One challenge is I had to be better than the men. When I started working with my current employer, I was the only woman in the corporate office. I had to work harder just to exist. Fortunately, the owner was a brilliant businessman who believed in me.

When you're a woman, you have to know what you're doing and convince the men that you know what you're doing. I had to work harder to justify to certain men that I should be at their level. Men can climb to the top just because they're men—they don't have to know what they're doing.

I've also had a full-time job at home and at work. I had to prove I could do both. My first priority was family, but I was determined to do a great job at work, too.

We've described bad girls as good girls who've had an "awakening." Did you have a defining moment or did you slowly "evolve" into a bad girl?

I had a defining moment. When my previous employer offered me less than a $1,000 salary increase to basically do two jobs, I realized he didn't respect women. He would never ask a man to do that. I told him to keep the job, and I planned ahead. I thought, "I won't stay here and be used." You should never, ever let yourself be taken advantage of, regardless of the price you pay. An ideal opportunity came along (two years later) and I took it.

Is there any wisdom you'd like to pass on about how you've done this?

Speak up. A woman's story is the last one that's heard. Some people say that women gossip. Well, men can be worse. Most of the women I've worked with speak out publicly, while the men manipulate behind the scenes.

You've also got to stick up for yourself and say what you mean. Over the years, I've never cared who was in the boardroom. I said what I had to say—I didn't care how it was received. Telling the truth is how I succeeded. Men I work with overproject—to make themselves look good. I say what's real. And I get heard because the owner benefits from hearing the truth.

I've seen women join the men and stoop to their level instead of rising above them. These women have no confidence in themselves. Remember, you're as good as or better than most men.

The Director: Amy Tinkham

(Age forty-four, choreographer/director, and mother of three)

At the age of twenty-two, Amy moved to Manhattan with no money, no connections, no boyfriend, and no job. Five hundred aerobics classes, two hundred-fifty cans of tuna, and three boyfriends later, Amy left for LA an accomplished modern dancer, having danced for Senta Driver and Nina Weiner. She moved from the low-paid world of modern dance to commercial and industrial dance. She hip-hopped, boogied, and bopped in MTV videos, commercials, and films. From dancer to choreographer and director, she now works with solo artists and groups, such as Mariah Carey, Paul McCartney, Britney Spears, and The Dixie Chicks on choreography and staging.

How does our bad girl definition apply to you?

I never thought I was good enough to be a good girl. I looked around and saw that I didn't fit into the mold. I've basically been a bad girl since first grade; I cheated on my reading tests to make it into the high-level reading groups. When I tried out for cheerleading, I pretended that I knew how to do gymnastics. I fell on my head during tryouts, but then I jumped up unscathed and yelled at the top of my voice. I showed that I had what it took to be a cheerleader. I was one for six years.

Amy faked it until she made it.

I faked it big-time when I was in my mid-twenties and I moved to LA from New York. I had been a modern dancer in New York, but in LA, I had to know jazz to land parts in MTV videos, films, and commercials. When I started auditioning, I was pretty bad. I pushed myself outside of my comfort zone, threw myself into the auditions, and learned what I had to do. I worked as a commercial dancer for ten years. Seven years ago, I decided I wanted to direct a short film, so I pretended that I knew how. I thought, Shit! I'd better figure this out before anyone finds out that I'm a total imposter. So, I bought a book about directing and read it as quickly as I could. I then directed a $40,000 short film that made it into the Sundance Film Festival.

Has your climb to the top included sweating and cursing?

Definitely. As a woman in my field, you have to fight a lot harder.

Most of the people who do well in my field are men, perhaps because you have to tell a whole lot of people what to do. But if you're a woman and not directing in a kind way, the people you're directing think you're PMSing or being dramatic. If you have a moment of indecision, they might call you something derogatory, like a deer in headlights. If a guy is taking a moment to reflect on his creative direction, people give him his space because he is having a creative block.

Amy has lots of stories about how challenging it is to be a woman in her line of work.

In projects where there's a guy above me, I often have to do all the work, but he gets the credit because he has the name.

Then there are guys who want pissing matches. Unfortunately, you might have to piss along with them. When a woman throws a fit, people will ask her to calm down, tell her she's being dramatic. But to establish your authority, you have to throw fits sometimes. And you'll find that people stop liking you when you do that, but you have to be okay with it. When I worked with Madonna, I watched her do it. She doesn't care what people think so much that— it's almost as if she gets off on people not liking her.

What about being a mother in your field?

You often have to deny motherhood. You can't ever use it as a reason for not doing something or for being late. People won't respect you; they'll think your attention is divided. When you're in the music and entertainment industries, you have to be hip and cool. It's just not hip to be a mother. But when I'm in charge, I sometimes bring my oldest son to rehearsals. People need to get used to the idea that mothers can be effective and competent in business.

Having such a successful work life, how do you juggle being a mom, too?

I'm not sure I balance it well. Maybe because there's not enough respect for women who do both. Women criticize each other. Stay-at-home moms are critical of working moms—there's a cloud of guilt and shame that goes with being a "good girl" mother. Good girl mothers do things like nurse for months, crush organic food, and use proper dialogue with their children. It's really killing women to have these standards. I think the bad girls of motherhood might not nurse at all, buy jarred food, and put their children in day care when they are six months old.

Amy's personal style is more stilettos than hiking boots.

I think I confuse people, especially men. I dress femininely, wear makeup and sexy outfits, but I am still powerful. It pisses men off; they are more threatened by sexy women. I'm a seducible female, but I'm also in control. Some men have no idea how to interact with you when you're both things. I'm not willing to give that up. I've considered looking asexual to get more respect, but then I wouldn't be true to myself.

Have other women been supportive of you? Who have been your cheerleaders?

Actually, it has been men—often more than women—who have supported me. The guys who have helped me along the way have been gay men, my husband, and my dad. Gay men see me as a diva. And my dad encouraged me in sports. I could run faster than boys until seventh grade. In fact, at my ten-year high school reunion, a guy came up to me and said he had always wanted to tell me that the guys in our class thought I had a penis because I could beat them at almost everything.

Amy, is there any wisdom you'd like to pass on to other women?

It's not unfeminine to be powerful or to be a bitch (confronting, raising your voice, speaking the truth, and being direct). You can be aggressive and still be really sexy and beautiful. If it turns men off, those are men you don't want to be with anyway.

If your objective is to get a guy, you won't get one. If your objective is to do whatever the hell you want to do, really cool wonderful guys will come into your life. The guys who aren't threatened by power will show up. If you spend your whole life on the other path, you'll get man after man who doesn't respect you.

And stop trying to please everyone. When I have to get a job done, there's so much pressure. There's only one way to get it done. There's not enough time to make everyone happy. In a way, it's liberating to know that—it releases me from the responsibility of pleasing everyone.

The Troublemaker: Trisha Flynn

(Age early sixties, journalist, and mother of three)

Trisha is just barely a product of a Catholic school upbringing—she managed to get herself expelled from every school she ever attended. What got her into trouble? Arguments over religion. As she explains it, "That Garden of Eden story, a first grader wouldn't buy it. What, do snakes talk? It never did make any damn sense to me. Why would Eve do such an evil thing? I suspect she was bored out of her tree."

Trisha's twin passions are theology and physics. As she sees it, religion is the bottom line for the position of women in society. She's written about religion, contraceptive rights, and other controversial topics in her columns in the Denver newspapers the *Rocky Mountain News* and the *Denver Post*.

Trisha, you've dedicated several columns to the reproductive rights issue. How did this come about?

When Reagan came into power, the whole reproductive rights issue was on the table. The language I used to write about this issue got me into trouble. The ironic thing is the papers wouldn't have hired me if I hadn't written the way I did: I was a mouthy housewife. I never tried to fool anybody. Women bitching and complaining with a sense of humor is "darling."

When she wrote about more than "cutesy mommy" stuff, she got flack from her editor.

In an article about contraceptive rights, I used the word "vagina." The paper wouldn't print it. We're talking about someone regulating what goes in and what goes out of a woman's body, not the common nostril or armpit. Being outrageous and political is male territory. When I entered this territory, my male editors sometimes took offense. When I had women editors, they printed my articles untouched.

Trisha, you're a much-honored journalist, having been nominated twice for Pulitzers and won tons of awards. To what do you attribute this success?

My columns got through because of women editors.

They wouldn't send my column upstairs (inevitably to a male editor). They'd put it through and let me take the shit. Most women are not real confrontational. I am. I'm not afraid of a scene or screaming.

Trisha was also popular with women, which is why she says she wasn't fired.

Some women bought the paper just for my column. I wasn't publicized. The *Post* did a name recognition survey and I came in as number two (after seven years at another paper).

I believed that most women thought and believed what I did—they just wouldn't have said it in the same way. The comments I got the most were, "You say exactly what I think." In my opinion, what was going on was just that. Most women don't put it straight out there. They sugarcoat it—like southern women.

You say that what you wrote about was mainstream. So why did you get into trouble?

I was and am mainstream, but I'm willing to speak out. What I wrote about wasn't known to be mainstream, but it was. For example, Catholic women use birth control and have as many or more abortions than the average American woman. But they don't talk about it.

They go to church and send their kids to Catholic school, but they use birth control.

Any thoughts on feminism?

It's a four-letter word. And the younger generation doesn't identify with that generation. It's the whole "I'm a feminist but" thing. But this generation of women was born expecting so much more than we were.

Trisha, we say that bad girls can be powerful and feminine. Would you agree?

I've always worn stilettos and makeup. There is credibility in appearance. In most fields, if you want to open those doors, you have to look good.

We asked Trisha to pass on her bad girl wisdom.

I think women need to lower their expectations in love. Marriage should not be about getting a step up. There are young women who still want their partner to be superior to them: smarter, richer, better career. There's no reason why women can't be the breadwinners.

The Entrepreneur: Linda Alvarado

(Age fifty-five, president and CEO of Alvarado Construction, Inc., co-owner of the Colorado Rockies baseball team, and mother)

Linda Alvarado founded Alvarado Construction, Inc., in 1976. The company, which now employs 450 people, reportedly books more than $41 million in revenue a year, making it one of the largest commercial real estate development companies in the West. Linda is also the first Hispanic (male or female) majority owner of a major league franchise.

A nationally recognized speaker and advocate for Hispanic business issues, Linda has received numerous awards including the Sara Lee Corporation's Frontrunner Award and Revlon's Business Woman of the Year. Despite her list of achievements, she says she is still trying to eliminate four-letter words from her vocabulary, namely, *cook, wash,* and *iron.*

How did you become a bad girl?

I had five brothers, my own erector set, and parents who believed in me. My upbringing had a major positive impact on me becoming what you call a bad girl. My parents set high expectations and focused on achievement and encouraged my participation in activities that were not for "good girls," such as competitive sports. I really benefited from having five brothers. Being Hispanic and being a girl was a double whammy, but my parents raised me to accept obstacles in life. They taught me that race and gender were not excuses [for me not achieving my goals].

In our book, we say that women need to learn how to break the rules? Do you?

For me, finding ways to bend the rules has allowed me to thrive. It's what I've done to achieve my goals. Throughout my life, I've been the "first" and "the only" starting with my participation in competitive sports, followed by a college sports scholarship, construction jobs, work as a general contractor, founding a construction company, and becoming the owner of a sports franchise.

To what do you attribute your willingness to take risks?

Competitive sports. I played soccer with my brothers. One thing I've noticed about guys is that when they don't make the goal, but think that they've made the perfect kick, they say, "It wasn't my fault. The wind was blowing." They don't personalize it. Instead, they laugh it off.

A critical skill that women need to learn is how to win and lose. Women tend to personalize things. We blame ourselves and think we're not good enough or prepared enough. For example, when I was first bidding on construction projects, I thought that if I didn't get every project, there was something wrong with me. Now I know if you're picking up every project, you're leaving too much money on the table.

To take risks you can't be too caught up in what other people think of you. I'm okay with people thinking whatever they want to think. I had personal goals I wanted to achieve. I didn't want to get pulled down by everyone else's lack of perspective.

Did you have a turning point along the way, or a defining moment?

One experience that really shaped who I am was my job in college. When I was looking for a job, I noticed that there were jobs in construction and jobs in food service. I sure as heck didn't want to do food service, so I applied for the construction job. The guy who was accepting applications said, "Don't you understand that boys work construction and girls work food service?" Then someone else said, "Do you want this job just to make a point?" I said, "No, I want this job, because I think I could be good at it." And it was a prophetic moment—my entrée into construction. Little did I know that at that moment, I was launching my career. It was also just the beginning of the challenges I would face being a woman in a male-dominated field. Later, when I had my own company, I would use only my initials on bids for fear of losing a contract because of being a woman. I was essentially in hiding.

What obstacles have you encountered? How did you remove them?

Once I entered the field, I worked on construction sites in which there were no separate Sanilets for men and women. Inside the Sanilets, I would see pictures of me in various stages of undress, wearing a hard-hat—for safety. Of course it upset me, but I handled it by having a good sense of humor. There's nothing funny about sexual harassment, mind you; it's not tolerated in my company. But at the time, I thought humor was the best way to diffuse it.

I've run into people who will ask me what my father or husband does—indirectly asking me if they started the company and I just inherited it. They are implying that I haven't earned my achievements. Whether it's sexual harassment, subtle putdowns, or direct insults, there will always be people who try to make you feel inadequate. The important thing is to stay focused and tune out all the peripheral noise. If I had been distracted by that noise, I wouldn't have made it in construction. I was determined to make it because I liked the field.

Who have your supporters been? Have women been on your side?

When I first entered construction, both men and women criticized me. Women accused me of wanting to get a boyfriend, instead of recognizing my sincere passion for the field. Some people asked me what I was trying to prove. I discovered when there are no mentors, it's hard to keep the momentum going. I kept it going nonetheless. Then, when I started my own company, I couldn't find any other women who had started a construction company who could tell me how to package bids. Eventually, when men realized I was there to stay, they became my mentors and allies.

We advise women to develop a toolkit, one that includes sassy comebacks. What's in yours?

I think the strategy I rely on most is humor. When I do public speaking, humor gets people's attention and sets them at ease. People are comfortable when they see that you understand their perspective. I dealt with myths and stereotypes head-on. I'd say things like "Most people think that construction workers drink first thing in the morning. In reality, we don't start until eleven" and "In the field of construction, most people expect a 6-foot, 4-inch man to walk in the door, not a 5-foot, 5-inch woman."

Have you run into any problems being an attractive female in a male-dominated field?

When I go to a big meeting with people who don't know that the principle of Alvarado Construction is a petite Hispanic woman, they first offer their hands to the guys who are with me. They assume I'm just a junior associate. And I've had to be careful how I dressed. Wearing pink on a construction site would not have been a good idea. I'm more blue-collar than pink-collar anyway. What was important was dressing appropriately—not dressing like I had something to prove.

Any words of wisdom for aspiring bad girls?

When you are a pioneer—the first one through—you need to be a risk taker, have a sense of humor, and not take disappointments (I don't believe in failure) so seriously. You must have a sense of humor when you're deviating from the norm.

Also, women shouldn't sit around waiting for things to change. For example, lack of access to capital is a huge problem that prevents women from achieving what they can, particularly in business. The credit laws are biased. We need to take steps to proactively change these laws.

Do you have any final thoughts?

Well, I'd like to end with a story about something that happened on the opening day of a Rockies game. Before the game, officials, the other owners, and I walked out onto the field to greet the crowd; I was the only woman in the group. After the game, I received a letter from a Hispanic woman. She wrote: "You looked so small surrounded by a group of tall men. But as I looked at you, I had this feeling come across me. I thought of everything my Hispanic parents worked so hard to achieve, and the types of things we all dream of, and you suddenly grew in stature." This woman's words brought tears to my eyes as I realized how important taking those steps is for ourselves and others.

The Sex Worker: Jessica Engel (pseudonym)

(Age forty, prostitute, and single mom)

Jessica is a bad girl in the old school sense: She's a prostitute—at least part of the time. She's chosen this line of work out of a true affinity for it as well as the extra cash it affords her and her daughter. This bad girl has explored her sexuality to the fullest and has a lot to say about the power and beauty of female sexuality.

Jessica starts the interview by saying that we'll create controversy if we include her in our book.

I consider myself a feminist, but there are few feminists who respect what I do. Most of them believe I'm feeding into men's objectification of women instead of challenging their views. They see prostitution as being disrespectful of women. What they don't realize is that there are plenty of men who respect what we do.

So you're defending your profession even though it's illegal?

Yes. The truth is prostitution is a profession that should be recognized as valuable. And it will always exist as long as women suppress their sexuality and men are raised to believe they can't control themselves. If I could tell more people about what I do, it would help both women and men.

What do you mean by this? Is there a lesson here for budding bad girls?

Yes. Women should know that men go to prostitutes so they can fully express their sexuality. They can be free with us in a way they can't be with their wives or girlfriends. They can talk to a prostitute about what pleases them and not be told they're disgusting. I've learned things every woman should know.

Why do you think there are so many women out there who are not pleasing their men?

Most women have been raised to be prim and proper.

They've been taught that they don't have a wild sex drive, but they do.

Do you have any other words of wisdom to pass on?

Basically, the more women are empowered with their sexuality, the more they will be able to relate to men on that level and feel good about themselves. Women should get a book on biology. Study the male and female bodies. Study testicles and penises. Discover their bodies. Let go of rules and taboos that say it's not okay to do this. Women spend so much time on other things, their hair and nails, but how much time do they spend on their vagina? Get a mirror. Look at your vagina. Look at your clitoris—it's the most magical thing in the world. It's specially designed for your pleasure. That's its function. Get to know your breasts. Men love them and I have yet to meet one who prefers the fake ones to the real thing. [Plastic surgery] is an industry created by insecure women.

The Healer: Barbara Wilder

(Age sixty, intuitive healer and writer, and mother of one)

Barbara Wilder is an internationally acclaimed writer, teacher, and healer. In her groundbreaking book *Money Is Love* she shows women how to reconnect money to the sacred feminine and transform it into an agent for both personal and global prosperity. Her latest book, *Embracing Your Power Woman,* is a radical program that gives women in the second half of life the skills to recognize, embrace, and embody their innate feminine power. A dynamic speaker, she has appeared on numerous radio talk-shows including shows hosted by Shirley MacLaine and Uri Geller.

Barbara spent the first twenty years of her adult life in the motion picture business, first as an actor and later in production.

How does our definition of a bad girl apply to you?

I am definitely a bad girl. I never adhered to the belief systems taught to me. I've always believed women's position in the world had to change. I was part of the sexual revolution. We were changing from good girls to wild and sexy girls, creating the feminist era. And I've always loved cursing.

Being outspoken is something Barbara shares with Trisha and Margo.

Speaking out gets you in a lot of trouble. I worked in the film industry, the tightest knit boys' club on the planet. I was often the only woman in the room. One day in a budgeting meeting for a Roman Polanski movie, we discussed putting an extra $500,000 in the budget to fly actresses to Paris for auditions, where Polanski was living. (He couldn't risk travel to the U.S. because of his fugitive status on charges of drugging and raping a thirteen-year-old girl in 1977.) I joked, "Isn't it amazing that we have to spend an extra $500,000 because Roman Polanski likes to have sex with little girls?" None of the men responded. They were thinking: it could have been me.

You've written a book about money. What do bad girls need to know about it?

What women do traditionally in the world is not paid for, so we carry around the belief system that we're the slave class. If a woman was paid for the work she does at home, she would earn $300,000, according to a recent article in the *LA Times*. So to make money, you have to work at what men do. We must be part of the marketplace or we're not part of society. But women must find their own power being feminine, being women.

What are some myths you don't buy into?

That you have to have it all by forty. In our second half of life, women's potential is incredible. We're no longer encumbered by the day-to-day taking care of the family, and we have this incredible experience being mothers and nurturers. I see older women as the new leaders of the communities and the world.

Are there any myths that you've come up against?

An older women has no worth and power, and she's not sexy anymore. At one of my book signings, a promoter thought it was disgusting for me to show cleavage—I was wearing a low-cut dress. Women are desperately trying to hold onto youth because of this myth.

We say that bad girls have to find their courage. What is it that we fear?

The fear of being selfish. It *is* about us. If we're selfish, we get what we need and then we can provide for our loved ones. It's basic survival behavior. Even more powerful is the fear of breaking with the past. It keeps us from getting what we want. We worry that if we're too powerful, we won't be accepted by our sisters, or be attractive to men.

Any thoughts on feminism?

Exciting—we are in the process of moving past the idea that we're junior men in training. We're looking for and discovering what true feminine power is. But younger women are angry about feminism. They need to look to older women who have discovered what it's like to be truly powerful.

Advice for budding bad girls?
Go inside yourself to find your power. It's there; it just may be hiding. The world needs us out there with our power. Find your courage to look for it. It takes courage to find it. Explore what courage means. With that courage, you begin to take off the masks that prevent you from seeing who you really are. And one more thing: Kick butt and show cleavage!

And your favorite footwear is . . . ?
If I could walk in stilettos, I'd wear them. It's a gorgeous look. I wore stilettos as a young woman. I loved to show off my legs and painted toenails. My footwear of choice now is strappy, sexy sandals. Going for what you want is stylish and beautiful.

The Thinker: Jill Nagle
(Age forty-five, author of Whores and Other Feminists, *mother of one)*

Were you always bad or did you slowly evolve into a bad girl?
I think I was born "bad," insofar as bad means true to myself rather than to what others expect. An early

memory of this is in kindergarten, when pretty little Dawn Koch and I were seated on the floor in "circle," whispering to one another.

I told Dawn something secret. Mrs. Stirrup asked Dawn to repeat out loud what I had told her. I whispered to Dawn, "Tell her it's none of her business."

"That's none of your business, Mrs. Stirrup," Dawn said.

"Dawn! That's *rude!*"

"She told me to say it."

"Jill, that is *rude*. Go over and sit there in the corner."

I remember the feeling of being isolated from everyone, afraid and ashamed—and also sure that I was correct.

Although bad girls are influenced by the same myths as good girls, bad girls rebel against them. Is this true for you?

One thing that comes to mind is my and my partner's last names. For a variety of reasons, when we married, I kept my last name and my partner hyphenated his, tacking on mine. I have noticed that still, most male–female couples use the husband's last name exclusively.

Occasionally a woman will hyphenate, and rarely, both partners will hyphenate. So far I have not encountered a single man (other than my partner, though I have heard of others) who has altered his worldly identity in any way to reflect his partnership with a woman. It's overwhelmingly expected that only women will do this, because our identity is expected to be malleable according to which man we're with, a reflection of how we used to be men's property.

What are some ways you've noticed that women sabotage themselves?

I think women, myself included, feminist or not, can and do consciously choose and use any of a variety of "tools of the patriarchy" for their own ends. For example, pandering to stereotypes of style and beauty.

I think fem- (or femme-) identified queer women in particular have done a great job of reclaiming the trappings of traditional femininity as a source of power. I've found it feels easier to do this when trying to attract a butch woman rather than a bio-man, since male–female relationships are so often fraught with sexism.

In terms of the other stuff, I feel grateful to have worked through a lot of that, and I try to support other women in doing the same thing.

Have you been plagued by body image demons?

I feel pressure in feminist circles to pretend that because we know intellectually what crap these assumptions are made of, that therefore we are not affected by them. Bullshit. I don't know anyone who doesn't feel this stuff.

I think anyone who isn't affected by body image demons has either done years of daily work on themselves, has an exceptionally thick hide, or is asleep. I definitely feel affected personally by images of what I'm "supposed to" look like. I notice this most when I visit LA—other women have echoed this experience—within moments my body image plummets as the toothpick-thin, surgically-altered Barbies begin to populate my consciousness.

Do you have any sassy comebacks you'd like to share?

What comes to mind is a time I was making out with my girlfriend in front of our car, and a young guy entering a building yelled out, "Hey, which one of you's the guy?"

At first we bristled, but then recovered ourselves. One of us shouted back, "We take turns!"

Then we yelled to the guy, who was with a young woman, "Which one of you's the guy?"

Surprised, he also conferred with his girlfriend, then shouted back with a smile, "We take turns!" We all wound up giggling.

Any words of wisdom you can offer to aspiring bad girls?

Practice tuning into yourself and to others. Find solutions that meet everyone's needs. Exercise your sense of humor whenever possible. Get laid in the way you want. *You matter!*

Finally, when it comes to footwear—stilettos or hiking boots?

Hiking boots. Comfort takes the day.

The Artist: Deborah Fryer, PhD

(Age forty-three, documentary filmmaker and writer)

Since becoming a spelling bee champion at the age of twelve, Deborah has racked up an impressive list of accomplishments that include learning German and several romance languages, earning a PhD, finishing nine marathons, and traveling the world extensively making documentary films and making a difference. As a freelance filmmaker, she has worn nearly every hat in the business, contributing to almost two hundred documentaries and educational videos covering the environment, history, science, medicine, health care, energy, archaeology, and anthropology. Deborah wrote, produced, and directed *Shaken,* a documentary film about Parkinson's disease, which has been screened at film festivals throughout the United States and abroad, winning awards at the Beverly Hills, SCinema, and Newport Beach film festivals.

Have you always been a bad girl?

I think I evolved into one or changed back into one. I was dubbed a smartass at an early age—as early as age four by one of my mother's colleagues. My mother was putting together a lecture on art history and I was rattling off the names of the paintings and painters.

Throughout secondary school, I was put down for being gifted. In high school, there was even a Hate Deborah Club. I was the smartest kid in the school— taking college courses, showing up just for exams— and I was ostracized for it. My dad also told me that no one would ever marry me because I was too smart.

Did your bad girl go into hiding at this point?

Well, I dumbed myself down, and got quiet at school. I learned not to say certain things. Years later, I went through another devastating period. I stopped doing everything I liked—doing the *NY Times* crossword in ink, running marathons—to get my boyfriend's family to love me. I made myself less—smaller—to please them. He ended up leaving me, probably because I'd changed so much. Devastated, I went back to the things that fed me.

We'd call this classic sabotage behavior. What are some sabotage behaviors you've noticed in other women?

It makes me mad when women are indirect. They should speak up about what they want or need. Women with husbands and kids seem to be even less direct. Maybe it's part of the family dynamic. I have noticed that women often ask in a way that assumes the answer will be no, whereas men ask in a way that more often assumes the answer will be yes. Are men more confident? More demanding? Do they feel more entitled? Are women more sensitive? Deferential? Less confident? Or just unaware that they are doing this?

Here's an example of what I'm talking about. A couple is celebrating their tenth anniversary and looking for baby-sitters for their kids. Instead of asking me "Can you help me out this weekend?" my girlfriend asks, "Would you like to have our girls stay the weekend with you?" When it is asked that way—do I *want* to spend forty-eight hours baby-sitting two little kids—the answer is probably no. But if the question were asked directly, "Could you help me," the answer would be yes.

You took a leap—a big risk—choosing an artist's life.

I grew up without financial security, raised by a single mother without child support. I've never had a cushy life, so I guess I'm not afraid to go without.

How did you get started? Who helped you?

My mom helped me initially. She gave me the name of a cameraman at Nova in Boston, the Mecca of documentary filmmaking. I called him and from there I started freelancing—researching, writing, editing, holding the microphone for Nova, the History Channel, MSNBC, and PBS.

Are there any other unique challenges you've faced as a woman?

I left graduate school because of sexual harassment, and I never said anything about it. A male professor embarrassed me in front of other students with lewd comments, and tried to sabotage me, changing the format of the master's exam.

You left graduate school when you were attacked? What's the lesson here?

I was young. I wanted to crawl in a hole and hide. Self-blame is huge (for women). It's not your fault when something like this happens. I wish that women had role models that would help them to feel safe. Still, I didn't let sexual harassment stop my academic career. I researched other schools, and I waited until I could have a free ride somewhere else.

And now that you're older and stronger, how do you defend yourself against attacks?

Now I speak my truth. I say, "I'm feeling uncomfortable with the way you're treating me; I'd like you to stop."

We talk a lot about myths in this book? Which ones have you encountered?

That I've missed the boat, being forty-two without a husband and children. It seems that a woman is invisible without kids. But I've chosen this path. This realization came through a dream I had a few years ago when I was traveling all over the world making films for Nova. I was in an airport—I had a layover. Just as my plane was called, I noticed a gorgeous orchid exhibit. The question this situation presented was: Do I keep going or do I choose kids (or -chids)? I ran for the plane. I'm still conflicted about kids, but maybe my life is about birthing stories, books, and movies.

How have you done with the Double Black Diamond Challenge: money and love?

I have to start shifting my relationship with money. I'm in debt (from my film). I didn't pay attention to money until just last year. I wish I had started in my twenties. I should have invested in the nineties. I paid off low-interest student loans, when I could have taken that money and invested in stock. But I don't have any regrets about my path because it has been rewarding.

And love?

I'm not looking to be rescued (by a lover). I look for someone who honors, supports, and loves me. I'm in a place where I can be loved for being strong and smart. I don't have to make love to feel loved, but in the bedroom, I believe you should ask for what you want and get it. I don't wait around, hoping a guy will figure it out. I ask for what feels good, respectful, and playful. And I'll initiate.

Have you managed to avoid the body image demon that possesses most of us?

My yoga practice has helped me get over the body image stuff. It's hard to do. I teach yoga, and I'm not the skinniest one in class. But people have told me how strong and flexible I am. I've realized that's sexy, too. In yoga, it doesn't matter how long your legs are, your boob size; we all have things to work on.

What about the "F" word? Are you a feminist?
I am a feminist. We should absolutely be equal.

What wisdom can you offer to support aspiring bad girls?
I feel that my yoga practice has been the most transformational thing I have done. It was a doorway beginning with the physical that now encompasses the emotional and the spiritual and even the intellectual. A yoga practice makes your insides and outsides equally strong.

Deborah, we have to ask: hiking boots or stilettos?
Hiking boots. If you're going to climb Mount Kilimanjaro, Mount Olympus, Mount St Helen's, and Mount Washington, like I have, hiking boots are the only way to go.

Chapter Highlights

"Telling the truth is how I succeeded. Men I work with overproject—to make themselves look good. I say what's real."

—Margo Brunelli

"If your objective is to get a guy, you won't get one. If your objective is to do whatever the hell you want to do, really cool wonderful guys will come into your life. The guys who aren't threatened by power will show up."

—Amy Tinkham

"To take risks you can't be too caught up in what other people think of you. I'm okay with people thinking whatever they want to think."

—Linda Alvarado

"That Garden of Eden story, a first grader wouldn't buy it. What, do snakes talk? It never did make any damn sense to me. Why would Eve do such an evil thing? I suspect she was bored out of her tree."

—Trisha Flynn

"Kick butt and show cleavage!"

—Barbara Wilder

"My yoga practice has helped me get over the body image stuff. It's hard to do. I teach yoga, and I'm not the skinniest one in class. But people have told me how strong and flexible I am. I've realized that's sexy, too."

—Deborah Fryer

"Women spend so much time on other things, their hair and nails, but how much time do they spend on their vagina?"

—Jessica Engel

Stilettos Summit

I used to want the words "she tried" on my tombstone. Now I want "she did it."
—Katherine Dunham

About This Trail: The last leg of any journey is both exhilarating and exhausting. As you round the last corner and see the shining Stilettos Summit in the distance, you suddenly realize: I'm almost there!

Duration: The key to a quick ascent is to stop dragging your feet and leap ahead.

Distance: We don't have an exact number for you—just go the distance. This expression originated in boxing, where it means "to last for all the rounds that have been scheduled." Be the last woman standing.

Difficulty: Most trails steepen at the end, so the last leg is often the hardest. Just remember, if you've made it this far, you can make it all the way.

Backpack Essentials: Chocolate croissants and a steaming thermos of your favorite blend to celebrate your accomplishment.

What to Leave Behind: Fatalism—the belief that your life is fated to be just the way it is. Know this: What you believe is what you create. Our advice: Believe in yourself.

Early Pitfalls: You're on a life-changing journey, and you may experience some pain along the way. Change is not easy—it may feel as painful as a nasty breakup, a layoff, or even childbirth if you are birthing a whole new you. Just remember, change for the better is always worth the pain.

Trail Tip: Don't make this last leg a free solo. Surround yourself with women who are just as determined as you are.

At the Trail's End: You'll find that the choices you have made on your life path are more important than your choice of footwear. *Climbing Mountains in Stilettos* is about finding *your* path to fulfillment. Because when it comes to life and shoes, one size does not fit all.

We're nearing the end of our tale of two girls: the good one and the bad one. It's a true story with an unexpected ending—bad triumphs over good. It's the brave, bawdy, rebellious girl who gets the good things in life, while the much praised darling of teachers, parents, and employers gets less than she deserves.

What's your response to this twisted tale? What have you found out about being a woman and being yourself? Are you too good for your own good, or are you badder than these bad girl writers could ever imagine? Are you stuck in a crevasse, unsure of the direction you'd like your life to take? Or are you farther along, say, in the foothills, but lack the stamina to attempt the final ascent to your peak potential?

If you're like most women, you still have a few hills and valleys to trek through: your financial situation is troubling; your love life is withering; you can't exorcise the body image demons; and you can't fully possess your sassy self. What will it take to make it up the last switchback—to reach Stilettos Summit and stay there? It'll take a map—a personalized plan that takes you farther along the trail—to give you a leg up on the last leg of this journey.

Leave your Mary Janes at the trailhead. Slip them off, and we'll give you something more fitting for climbing to the top: heels! Each of these profiles builds from the training heel to the real deal—the stiletto. Mix and match or build up to the stiletto challenge.

Find the heel that fits or try them all out for size. Why limit yourself to one type of footwear? As the old saying goes, if the shoe fits, wear it.

Kitten Girl

The kitten is a training heel for the bad girl who has been in hiding. You'll be a little wobbly and shaky at first as you emerge onto the trail. The kitten heel is short, so it doesn't require a balancing act. This training heel will give you the feel of a lift without much threat of losing your balance and falling into a crevasse. Imagine a kitten transforming into a mountain lion. You will need to learn how to turn your cute squeaky meow into a roar. But like the Cowardly Lion, you may scare yourself at first.

If you're a kitten girl, your growth has been stunted by low expectations, lowly good girl rules and myths, and a severe lack of self-confidence. You lack the confidence to live life on your terms—not everyone else's—and to take on the things that truly interest you.

Fill your fanny pack.

Fill your pack with savory and stimulating treats for the trail ahead—to take you to the next level.

Mantra: Fear is just a four-letter word.

Physical: Improve your ability to defend. Try kickboxing or karate.

Emotional: Master boundary setting. Learn to use your claws when necessary.

Financial: Spend money on yourself. Buy something fun and frivolous, but nothing that breaks the bank.

Intellectual: Learn about Rosa Parks, a humble woman who made a big splash.

Film: *Erin Brockovich.*

Book: *In Her Shoes.*

Music: Destiny's Child or the lovely Beyonce.

Just for fun: Dress up as Cat Woman for your next costume party.

Fuel up on affirmations and meditation.

Put yourself in a peaceful, positive state of mind. Sit quietly and visualize your future. And then throughout the day, practice positive reinforcement with personalized mantras. Examples: I am a unique and wonderful woman, who seeks joy and fulfillment; I work hard and I deserve to be rewarded; I will make time for me today; I am going to take risks and find out what I'm capable of; I am a generous, warm person with many gifts to share; I have true friends and a loving family that supports me; I will nurture my physical and mental health today; I can succeed at new things; I will do my best; I can make a difference.

Secure your hold: practice self-confidence.
Each and every time you interact with someone, practice self-confidence. Stand up straight, look at the person you're talking to, lower your voice (no baby talk allowed), and speak with confidence, not questions.

Leap ahead: uncover the good girl and discover yourself.
The way to get moving on the trail is to root out the good girl programming lodged in a lobe of your brain, and create new neural pathways that help you discover your true self.

Leap #1: Uncover the good girl
What were you like as a girl before you entered adolescence? (If you don't remember, ask someone who does.)

Think about yourself as a young girl eight, nine, or ten years old. What were some of the good girl messages you received from your parents, teachers, and peers?

1. Good girls always:
2. Be a good girl and:
3. Good girls never:

Leap #2: Discover yourself
Make a list of all the things that you are passionately dedicated to and curious about. What subjects would you like to study intensively? What activities would you like to get involved in? What career path do you truly wish to pursue? Perhaps you're a girl who likes to start up things—as a political organizer or an entrepreneur. Or do you love to work with people—making things happen or making a difference? Maybe you're most blissed out when you're doing research and writing—we can relate to that! Or would you be happier doing something physical or outdoors? Create your discovery list below.

My Discovery List:

_____

_____

Cuban Girl

Cuban girl is a rebel. As Cuban Girl, you will embody the spirit of revolution. You're on the trail, but you lack zest and passion because you have given in to the rules of the good girl for so long. And at this point in your life, you don't see an obvious way to turn things around. Changing your life midstream just isn't a possibility, is it? Yes, it is. But you'll have to be patient because you've got a lot of work ahead of you. In the words of a huge seventies musical talent, Sister Sledge: "Here's what we call our golden rule: Have faith in you and the things you do. You won't go wrong." And you won't go wrong if you continually remind yourself that there's no one else like you in this world.

The Cuban heel will give you courage to be a scofflaw and an outlaw. Soon you'll be smoking on the trail in your Cubans!

Fill your fanny pack.

Devour goodies that stimulate your mind and heat up your body.

Mantra: This revolution will be televised!

Physical: Put fire in your feet and try tango, salsa, or rumba.

Emotional: Play the devil's advocate.

Financial: Contribute money to a cause that incites passion and purpose.

Intellectual: Learn about how Communism and Marxism influenced Frida Kahlo's paintings.

Film: *Volver.*

Book: *How the Garcia Girls Lost their Accents*
Music: Shakira.
Just for fun: Paint the town red. Dress up in vibrant red and learn to tango!

Fuel up on spiritual and emotional hot chili peppers.

Seek out activities, people, and places that incite your passion and make your blood boil—in a good way.

Secure your hold: be passionate.

Watch a friend, acquaintance, or celebrity who is fiery and outspoken; then practice setting a room on fire, and we're not talking arson.

Leap ahead: be revolutionary.

To be a revolutionary you sometimes have to stand alone; you're toppling the status quo. Move to the center of controversy rather than avoiding it on issues that matter to you. In the past you may have suppressed a thought or opinion because it was controversial; now don't hold back.

Leap #1: Give a speech

Share your passion for a topic, person, or political cause and have fun doing it. Haven't you secretly fantasized about giving an "Oscar-worthy" speech to an adoring crowd? Well, now's the time to give it a try. Brainstorm speech topics and possible speechmaking opportunities. Here are some ideas:

- Host an evening gathering to share a slideshow of your latest travel adventure.
- Write a toast for a friend's wedding, birthday dinner, or anniversary party.
- Speak out on an issue you care deeply about at a city council meeting, a political rally, or a PTA meeting.

Leap #2: Try a hot workout

Raise your fitness level and your sexy quotient with these steamy workouts.

Zumba: A high-energy workout invented by Columbian Beto Perez. Zumba combines calorie-burning, body-blasting aerobics with the hot, sexy styles of the most popular Latin rhythms.

The Striptease Workout: This workout will work you up to performing a first-rate pole-dancing routine. Enjoy sensual floor work, powerful hip work, and pole tricks.

Stiletto Strength: A thirty-minute strengthening and stretching class geared toward developing the physical skills needed to stay lifted and balanced in your favorite pair of Choos.

Wedge Girl

As Wedge Girl, you are wedged between good and bad. You haven't decided which way to go, which is why you need wedge heels. They will lift and shift you forward on the trail. This heel provides the stability of the ridge, but will give you practice with the slope and height. Indecision may stall you on the path, but don't give up. You're at a crossroads where many trails merge; you must use the impetus of the wedge to shift you forward in the direction of the summit.

Wedge Girl has a limited perspective on what it takes to be a bad girl. You're a victim of "don't know much about bad girl history," and you can't walk your talk. You suspect your life is off balance, but you haven't found a way to regain it and shift forward. There are two major challenges for Wedge Girl: (1) stop letting everyone around you suck up your time and resources, and (2) start taking care of yourself. Here's what we suggest for you:

Fill your fanny pack.
Fill up your pack with supplies that that will sustain you.

Mantra: Not deciding is deciding.

Physical: Enhance your stance and strength by doing yoga, Pilates, or weight-lifting.

Emotional: Shift the balance of power in a romantic relationship by being the first to say "I love you."

Financial: Take control of your budget by deciding how to invest your money.

Intellectual: Volunteer to lead a group, such as a hiking or community club. You get to make all the decisions.

Film: *The Virgin Queen*, a drama about the life of one of Britain's greatest monarchs, Elizabeth I. Her femininity baffled and threatened the male order of Renaissance England for more than forty years.

Book: *The Bitch in the House*

Music: Lauryn Hill.

Just for fun: Pretend you're the film director for a sex scene, only in this scene you're also the leading lady!

Fuel up on selfishness.

Do you suffer from a case of selflessness, putting everyone else's needs first and yours last? Let's do a quick reality check and find out. If you answer yes to any of these questions, you've got to add selfishness to your survival kit.

1. I don't have any time for self-care—for exercise, meditation, a relaxing bath, or just a little down time.

2. I've been working half my life, but I don't have anything (material) to show for it.
3. The people I take care of rarely, if ever, take care of me.
4. I'm always playing second fiddle—at work and at home.

Secure your hold: practice saying no.

In order to carve out time for you and your life, you're going to have to start saying no. Every time someone tries to steal your time and attention for something you really don't want—and you most certainly don't need—to do, you've got to say no. If you don't, you'll never gain the foothold you need to take the next step.

Leap ahead: learn your lessons and walk the talk.

You're on the trail, but do you know where you're going? In life, every step forward seems to come with one step back. Try walking in the shoes of living legends. The steps they've taken make it easier for all of us to get ahead. They've broken the trail and provided trail markers to make the climb easier for us.

Leap #1: Take the Living Legends Quiz

Here are just a few women whose lives will guide you in the right direction. Do you know what they're famous for?

1. Barbara Walters made television history by
   a. co-anchoring a nightly network news program, *ABC Evening News*
   b. exposing her right breast during a Super Bowl halftime show
   c. hosting the hit reality show *Date My Mom*

2. Rita Moreno will go down in entertainment history for
   a. starting the *Macarena* dance craze
   b. locking lips with Madonna at the 2003 VMAs
   c. being only the second person to have won an Oscar, a Grammy, a Tony, and an Emmy

3. Madeline Albright's most acclaimed political accomplishment is
   a. being pretty funny on *The Daily Show*
   b. serving as secretary of state during the Clinton administration
   c. telling VP Dick Cheney to "go f— yourself."

4. In 1988, Toni Morrison's book *Beloved*

   a. won a Pulitzer Prize for fiction

   b. was an Oprah's Book Club selection

   c. edged out John Grisham's *A Time to Kill* to claim the number one spot on the *New York Times* bestseller list

5. In a historic battle of the sexes, Billie Jean King

   a. beat out Matthew on *Survivor: Amazon* to win the $1 million prize

   b. defeated Bobby Riggs in an exhibition tennis match

   c. lopped off her opponent's penis with a tennis racket

6. As _____, Nancy G. Brinker has given all women a reason to run a 5k.

   a. the creator of the sports bra

   b. the majority shareholder of Krispy Kreme stock

   c. the founding chair of the Susan G. Komen Breast Cancer Foundation and the *Race for the Cure*

7. Oprah Winfrey worked herself up from

   a. Mouseketeer to being one of the highest grossing artists of all time

   b. radio station reporter to becoming the first African American woman billionaire

c. stockbroker to becoming the CEO and founder of a powerhouse media company centered on the domestic arts

8. Fashion all-star Vera Wang's career path took an interesting turn when she traded in
   a. competitive ice-skating for designing upscale wedding gowns
   b. café singing for designing classic couture and an eponymous fragrance
   c. being a princess for founding a fashion house and creating the "wrap dress"

Answers: 1. a; 2. c; 3. b; 4. a; 5. b; 6. c; 7. b; 8. a

Leap #2: Imagine yourself as a bad girl

If you can dream it, you can become it. Imagine being the ultimate bad girl in your day-to-day life; what would that look like? How would your daily interactions with people change? How would your life change? Write a story (or two or three) starring yourself as the bad girl, and then start walking your talk!

Use at least one of the following sentences:

- I floored him with a sassy comeback.
- And ever since then, the Neanderthal men at work tiptoe around me.
- I dropped the polite act and told them what I really thought.

- As soon as I stopped using disclaimers, I started getting respect.
- I showed him what I really wanted him to do—and he did it very well.
- "You have two choices: give me a raise or find someone to replace me—today."
- For the first time in my life, I didn't volunteer to do what no one else wanted to do.
- The rule at my house is, you do the dishes or you don't eat.
- Ever since I lost all his clothes, my husband's been doing the laundry.

Leap #3: Saying yes to no

Take a moment to think about the word *no*. It is a small word with a big attitude. It is made up of just two letters—*n* and *o*. It is easy to pronounce, and it has a powerful finality to it. Think of all the benefits of saying no.

Saying no
- allows you to hold on to personal power
- helps you save time, money, and energy
- demonstrates self-confidence
- allows you to set the terms
- encourages others to share in responsibilities
- prevents you from stretching yourself too thin
- prevents meltdowns that deplete your vitality

- lets you know who your real friends are
- prevents you from harboring resentment
- takes care of you

If you're worried about letting others down, have you ever thought that letting someone else down may mean bringing yourself up?

Platform Girl

Platform shoes take you to new heights with the added benefit of stability. Platform Girl sometimes suffers from the slump syndrome—a slumping self-esteem or body image, or the glass ceiling. Platform shoes increase your stature and give you the lift without the instability of the stiletto.

As the trail steepens and energy wanes, Platform Girl feels weighed down by excess baggage. The key to your success is to lighten your load and increase your stature. If you have made it this far, you may have discarded useless items such as baby talk and toxic boyfriends, but you're still clinging to unrealistic ideals, and you occasionally slip into sabotage behavior without realizing it. Here's what we suggest for you:

Fill your fanny pack.
Savor these sweet treats.

Mantra: I'm big and bad! No one can make me feel small.

Physical: Add height and stature by trying Rolfing or chiropractic.

Emotional: Take up space by hogging a train seat or proposing your ideas in a meeting.

Financial: Ask for a raise, fight for a bonus, or let someone else foot the bill.

Intellectual: Learn about *The Pirate Queen.*

Film: *Truth or Dare.*

Book: *Eat, Pray, Love.*

Music: Defying Gravity, *Wicked Soundtrack.*

Just for fun: Take a stretch limo through the city. See how it feels to take up so much space.

Fuel up on renewed sense of purpose.

Fight fatigue with a renewed sense of purpose. Remind yourself that your hard work will pay off and it will help other women get on the trail.

Secure your hold: reduce clutter.

Clear your path by reducing the clutter in your life. It's blocking both your view and your progress. Try to see clearly the thoughts and actions that are littering your path, and then get rid of them!

Leap ahead: lighten your load.

A seasoned backpacker knows to pack only the bare essentials: food, water, shelter, and a first-aid kit. Adding needless weight will only slow you down and wear you out. It's time to take inventory of the beliefs and behaviors that are holding you back. Hold onto only those beliefs and behaviors that will take you to the summit!

Leap #1: Let go of your beloved myth

A beloved myth is a sparkling fantasy that you treasure so deeply that it's dulling your appreciation for and enjoyment of your real life. Your failure to make this dream materialize is taking its toll on your self-confidence and self-esteem. What beloved myth are you still holding onto? Is it the one about a cellulite-free body being your only entrée to nirvana? Or the one that says your beauty must be frozen in time or you'll lose your worth? Are you still convinced your life is not a fairy tale without Prince Charming and 2.1 picture-perfect children? Or that your partner is less than perfect if he doesn't outpace on his career path?

What is *your* beloved myth? Why not replace it with an appreciation of your luscious reality? Get this down on paper and then get on with your life.

My Beloved Myth:

_____

_____

My Luscious Reality:

_____

_____

Leap #2: Sink the last sabotage

Eliminating sabotage behavior from your pack will give you a huge energy boost. Toss it out once and for all, and you'll float to the next level of bad girlhood. In our own experience and in our research with other bad girls, we have identified the top three "hard to sink" sabotage behaviors. Have you sunk all sabotage behavior once and for all? Prove it. Tell us your sink strategy for each of the following:

Sabotage #1: Objectify yourself

Our example: When people comment on my body, I don't join in. I refuse to talk about my body parts, my size, or my shape.

My Sink Strategy:

_____

_____

Sabotage #2: Toot your own horn
Our example: I let my boss know what my accomplishments are, either by spelling them out or working them into a conversation.

My Sink Strategy:

_____

_____

Sabotage #3: Avoid the imposter syndrome
Our example: Though it makes me nervous each time I do it, I dive into new challenges, pretending I know what I'm doing.

My Sink Strategy:

_____

_____

Stiletto Girl

Stiletto Girl is nearly at Stilettos Summit. You are ready for the stilettos challenge. You know life is a balancing act, but you are mastering it. As Stiletto Girl, you are smart, sassy, and super-sexy. Consequently, you're often criticized for behaving like "you're all that." Well, you are all that! Women and men should start looking up to you instead of cutting you down, withdrawing their support, or backstabbing you at every opportunity. It's no wonder that you are occasionally plagued by doubt. Who wouldn't be? Without support and positive reinforcement, we all wither instead of grow.

But you should know you're not alone. The pack may have thinned at this stage of the climb, but there are women who are scrambling to join you. Teaming up with supportive, loyal girlfriends will help you overcome any lingering doubts you have about your flawless performance.

Fill your fanny pack.

Stack your pack high with vertigo-inducing delectables.

Mantra: Invoke my inner stiletto.

Physical: Trapeze, tight-rope walking, juggling, other circus arts.

Emotional: Go out on a limb with someone by sharing a secret you've never shared with anyone.

Financial: Make a high risk, potentially high return investment.

Intellectual: Make international travel plans and commit to survival-level language proficiency before you arrive.

Film: *The Devil Wears Prada.*

Book: *The Sisterhood of the Traveling Pants.*

Music: Dixie Chicks

Just for fun: Have a stilettos sprinting contest with your girlfriends. Then pamper yourselves with a foot massage and pedicure.

Fuel up on partnerships.

While many of the bad girls who attempted this climb before us did it alone, we don't have to. Forget the solo performance; it's time for us to seek out partnerships and support each other.

Secure your hold: define teamworthy.

A team succeeds when its teammates work hard, support each other, and believe they can win. Girls above treeline must team up, actively recruiting teamworthy girlfriends. What makes a girl teamworthy? We suggest you look for the following traits in a recruit:

- She cheers on her teammates.
- She wants everyone to win.
- She's genuinely happy when her teammates succeed.
- She welcomes new members.
- She generously shares her gifts.
- She mentors the newbies.
- She's supportive, offering help and comfort for those who need it most.
- She works hard and expects the same from everyone else.

Leap ahead: separate the wheat from the chaff and build a nourishing network.

You don't have to go it alone on the last leg of the journey. Bring a team of winners and an exclusive club of stiletto-loving bad girls with you!

Leap #1: Build your summit team

Imagine that you are part of an all-female expedition to Mount Everest, and that you have made it to the final camp. With one last push, you could conquer the notoriously tricky summit. However, the trek from base camp has left you depleted, and you have spent the last two nights in the oxygen-deprived death zone, waiting out a storm. When the expedition leader calls everyone together to tell you that there's a break in the weather and it's time to form summit teams, which women will you team with for the final ascent? Which of these women will ensure that you make it to the top? The one who carried your pack when you were ready to quit, or the one who expected you to be her sherpa? The one who generously shared her oxygen supply, or the one who hoarded hers? The one who helped you up when you took a nasty tumble, or the one who stepped over you and raced ahead?

While our daily life may not be as intense and potentially life-threatening as an Everest expedition, the women we team with in life either lift us up or keep us down. To make it on this last leg of the journey, you must choose your friendships and partnerships wisely. Your safety and survival may depend on it. Think about all the women in your life—your friends, family, and coworkers. Which ones would you choose to accompany you on a life-threatening climb? Which ones would you leave at base camp? List your summit team members below, and describe the traits that have earned them a spot. Try to come up with at least five women.

My Summit Team Members   Their Qualities

_____

_____

_____

_____

_____

Leap #2: Start a club
How can you keep the momentum going while at the same time infusing other aspiring bad girls to reach their peak potential? Start a stilettos club. Here are a few tips for getting started:

How to launch your own stilettos club.
1. Invite teamworthy girls.

2. Create a fashion code: stilettos or hiking boots?
3. Set a regular day for club meetings: the third Monday of the month.
4. Alternate leading the group: everyone should learn how to lead.
5. Discuss *Climbing Mountains in Stilettos* (see the book club discussion questions).
6. Do the activities in the book together.
7. Make up your own activities.
8. Attend the *Climbing Mountains in Stilettos* workshop. (See our website for cities and dates.)
9. Invite Ann and Carol to join you—really! We do a lot of traveling and we'd love to strap on our stilettos and head out to one of your meetings.
10. One final note: Visit our website and tell us what you think. Share your reactions and ideas. Tell us what activities you loved; which ones you weren't so fond of. Most important, we want to build a network of bad girls who climb mountains shoulder to shoulder. That way, we'll never lose our way, run out of fuel, lose our grip, or fail to summit. And don't forget—bring your own stilettos.

Stilettos Book Club Questions

- What does the title of this book mean to you?
- Do you view feminism as the "F" word?
- Does "invoke your inner stiletto" resonate with you?
- What good girl rules have you lived by?
- How have the good girl rules cramped your style?
- Discuss the good girl rules you would like to shatter.
- What women of history inspire you?

- Which woman featured in this book do you identify with the most?
- What scared your bad girl into hiding?
- If your bad girl went into hiding, did you have a slow or fast and furious awakening?
- What prompted your bad girl to awaken from her slumber? (We know it wasn't a kiss from a prince.)
- What do you think about the claim "free your mind and your body will follow"?
- Why are our luscious bodies such battlegrounds?
- Are you hopeful about women regaining a healthy body image?
- Why is money such an emotional trigger for women?
- Is money a trigger for you?
- Were you surprised that 90 percent of working women in the United States make less than $50,000?
- Were you surprised when you learned that the United States has the highest rate of women living in poverty? What can we do about it?
- Is your credit card situation out of control? What is your plan to get out of debt?
- Have you ever hosted or been to a sex toy party?
- How do you define sleeping around and how do you feel about it?

- What's your favorite sassy comeback?
- What does the younger generation need to know about how far women have come in the last century?

Pink Past to a Rosy Future

I fell off my pink cloud with a thud.
—Elizabeth Taylor

Ballet slippers, tutus, ribbons, cotton candy, bubble gum, little girls' wardrobes, and the three little pigs are just a few pink things that evoke innocence, sweetness, and purity.

The pink palette's rosy hues of salmon, coral, hot pink, fuchsia, and blush are also delicious and daring, but they pale alongside their close cousin, red.

Red is the color of fire, blood, lust, passion, red-hot chili peppers, strength, and power. Red grabs attention, urges action, warns of danger, and infuses people with energy. With this vibrant color, we roll out the red carpet and paint the town red.

Does this mean that a bad girl must forsake pink for red? Or that a good girl can be rooted out by the amount of pink in her wardrobe? No, not really. If you look around, you'll find that most women don't even wear pink much. And if you ask a woman what her favorite color is, she's more likely to choose purple than pink or red. But pink can be a symbol of strength: the inverted pink triangle symbolizes gay pride, and the pink ribbon is worn to raise awareness about breast cancer. So it's not just sugar, spice, and everything nice. Rather than being a symbol of girlhood, girliness, or the ultimate in femininity, we think the color pink is like a woman: beautiful, complex, and rich in meaning and history.

Carol and Ann used to be good girls. They pleased their parents. They delighted their teachers, and they adhered to the rigorous moral teachings handed down to them through Catholicism and Presbyterianism. Their bad girlhood was not easily won and they have "pink" stories to show for it.

Queen of Hearts and Powder Puff Football—Ann

In high school, I was in a sorority called the Queen of Hearts. The name sounds benign enough—conjuring up images of pink hearts and girls in sparkling tiaras.

The club was a sought-after sorority for popular girls that was based on fame, shame, blame, and games. As pledges (fledgling members) we were required to be popular, perky, and carry pledge sacks full of candy to school. We were mandated to greet actives in the hallways and stand at the ready for their commands. When they would shout *"Air raid!"* we had to get down on all fours and say, "I know my heart. I know my mind. I know that I stick out behind. Watch me wiggle." To top it off, we had to shake our butts in the air for all passing high schoolers to see. Why girls would intentionally disgrace each other with militaristic hazing rituals, I'll never understand.

Being in this sorority was a so-called privilege, but it brought me mostly humiliation. On one occasion, I was berated at a meeting for not correctly greeting an active. She went ballistic because I didn't give her the "hello" she wanted. I was so upset, I practiced my "hellos" for weeks.

We played "powder puff" football—a pink, frilly name for a brutal sport. I was always looking for the powder or the puff, but the only thing puffy was my face after I was slammed to the ground as a running back.

It was "flag" football in which girls with black stripes painted under their eyes would knock each other down in the muddy grass and then grab the tackled girl's flag. I went along with it, but felt all the while as if we could be doing something more civilized—something more useful than emulating blood-thirsty men in mud.

I learned early that the hearts, the pink, the powder, and the puff were all a front for putting and keeping each other down. I saw that many girls couldn't be trusted with your secrets or your heart. It took me decades to unlearn this early lesson.

If my bad girl wasn't in hiding before I joined the Queen of Hearts, she was definitely in hiding afterward. Shouldn't a high school girls' club teach girls to be bigger, better, and badder than they are?

No Perky Points in Pink Collar Politics—Ann

I've always been a reserved person, rather on the serious side of things, not a typical American gal. Certainly not the girl next door. I didn't even make the final cuts in cheerleading tryouts. Rather than being perky, I'm pouty; rather than bouncy, I'm flat; rather than outgoing, I'm an introvert; rather than looking on the bright side, I dwell on darkness. Oh and my mother says I wear too much black—that I must diversify my wardrobe. Am I in mourning? Well, yes, because I'm trapped in a pink-collared world. My nature and attitude have not served me well at work. The boys' club would rather see a perky, bubbly, bright-eyed serving female in muted pastels than one who is brooding, dark, and doesn't see their greatness and worship them accordingly. I was never good at faking. Not even orgasms. The boys' club couldn't tell the difference anyway.

There was a woman at work who worked her way up the ladder with well-sculpted hairdos, a Miss America pageant smile, and Stepford wife clothing. Yes, lots of prints with itty-bitty flowers. Once an executive secretary, she's still one after seventeen years—only now with a fancy title and a big salary. An obsessive-compulsive type, she'd spend hours composing two-page emails about how to perfect the art of making and serving coffee and pastries to Korean executives. Once, I actually heard her say to the president, a man whose ego she strokes like a lap cat, "Charles in charge, what can I do for you?" Charles in charge? Nothing like this could ever come out of my mouth, even if I was being held hostage by the Christian militia with their homemade pipe bombs. (Might I suggest homemade Jesus is Lord cookies instead?)

But my low score on the perkiness scale did not serve me well with Charles in charge and his Korean golfing buddy, Mr. Lee, the VP. Once, before Mr. Lee had any idea what my position in the organization was, he approached my desk, stood over me, and began to talk at me. I looked at him blankly and he repeated his words. "Yes, I know, I heard you the first time," I said. He demanded, pacing back and forth, "Type this into your computer." Ah, I'm supposed to "dick-tate," I thought to myself.

I put my fingers to the keyboard and, with a belligerent look on my face, began to type his words. I never sent the letter and not so accidentally lost the file. He never spoke to me again.

Then, I heard through the grapevine that the president was not happy with my performance. Of course, he didn't have the nerve to tell me to my face, so he just relied on the insidious rumor mill. I didn't hear anything specific or concrete, rather just fourth-hand comments that when you hear them have the embellishment of creative authorship many times over. Wanting to cut down on the collegial creativity factor, I went straight to the president myself—ready to receive constructive feedback about my performance. When I asked him what the problem was, he, being an exacting Ivy

League type, chose his words carefully. He said, "We need program specialists who are bubbly." Then, restating his comment so that it was more concise, he said, "We need bubbles for program specialists." I sat there dumbfounded as the words echoed in my mind: bubbles for program specialists. My mind quickly conjured up an image of the president's favorite program specialist, a stern, sardonic, dour Ukrainian guy who hadn't cracked a smile since Perestroika. Bubbles—huh? If he's a bubble, then I'm the queen of bubble machines. But shame gripped me as I, once again, faced the reality that I hadn't lived up to the American bubble standard. I suppose this goes back to what I was saying about perkiness. I never did make cheerleading, and now there was no hope for me as a bubble in the workplace.

I have nothing against bubbles. In fact, bubble baths are quite exquisite. Blowing bubbles with bubble gum, albeit sophomoric, is divine irreverence. And making bubbles with a bubble maker inspires childlike mischievousness. Perhaps I'm being a bubble-brain here, but what do bubbles have to do with performance?

Scrumptious Pink Coconut Snack Thing—Carol

At age thirteen, the walls closed in on my identity. I was growing breasts—barely—evolving into this new thing: a body, an object, a sum of my weight and height. And then I got my period, which came later than everyone else's. I grew more apprehensive about my new condition by the day.

While playing after school one afternoon, I challenged my younger brother to a fifty-yard dash, and he beat me for the first time ever! This was the scrawny younger brother I regularly wrangled with and usually dominated. Now he could run faster than me. I was devastated. I felt certain that my life was over, unless I somehow regained a foothold. I couldn't do anything about the new identity that was being pushed on me or the changing body that was failing me, so I took control over the one thing I could: food. I counted calories. I weighed myself religiously. I forsook bread for apples and sweets for glasses of Tab. I even gave up sugar for a whole month. I was slipping into an eating disorder and slowly wasting away.

Now don't take this the wrong way. Anorexia has its perks, the primary one being it doesn't require any knowledge of good nutrition. My limited knowledge of the food pyramid led me to feast on junk food intermittently during my famine. My favorite weekend lunch consisted of one slice of American cheese (the individually wrapped slices) and one scrumptious pink coconut-covered snack thing. Luckily, among my four siblings with voracious appetites, there wasn't any competition for these sticky works of art. (How do they make food such a pretty shade of pink?)

What knocked the sense back into me? How did I get out of pink puffy snack hell and back to a healthy life? Well, I eventually ran out of steam. Adolescence is tough enough without walking around half-starved. Adjusting to a new school and healing a broken heart probably didn't help, either. Life's knocks can sometimes knock sense into us and that was the case for me.

So, do I count calories today? Do I eat pink things that don't have names? No, no to both! Instead, I try to stay strong and healthy. I've also devoured dozens of cooking and nutrition books over the years and realized that eating lots of colors—not just pink—is a healthier way to go.

I Dream of Jeannie Halloween— Carol

Back in the fall of 1976, I began my annual preparations to create my Halloween costume. Holed up in my bedroom for hours on end, I scribbled ideas in my diary, trying to come up with something new, something bold, and someone I'd never been before. The previous year I was a smash hit as a movie star: fake fur, mom's stylishly frosted bobcut wig, a giant psychedelic plastic ring, and generous globs of blue eye shadow and red lipstick. The year before that, I was a hippie chick decked out in "Indian" moccasins, a tie-dye headband, giant hoop earrings, and corduroy patchwork bell-bottoms. The year before that, I got Mom to pierce my ears so I could be a "real" gypsy. My costume included *pierced* gold coin earrings and a matching necklace, a hot-pink headscarf, and a fire engine red ruffle dress with oversized polka dots. Whom did I want to be this year? Whose shoes did I want to walk in if only for one night? I asked myself. And then it came to me, as if in a dream. Jeannie. I wanted to walk in *I Dream of Jeannie*'s pointy pink slippers—even if the forecast called for light snow.

It never occurred to me that I would have a hard time coming up with an all pink harem outfit. My wardrobe had a pink theme. I was a hot pink—a daring choice for a little girl if I may say so myself. And I was living in a sea of pink. My bedroom décor was to die for: pink bedspread, pink sheets, pink blanket—even a pink scatter rug. As far as I knew, pink was everyone's—or at least every girl's—favorite color.

As I dug through my mother's dresser drawers (a great place to look for Halloween ideas), I found one pink treasure after another: a gauzy pastel pink scarf, a sparkling pink jewel-studded crown (was my mother a princess?), and a perfect pair of hot-pink pointy slippers to create an authentic Jeannie look. I didn't have to rub a genie's bottle to get my wish: I'd come up with yet another winning Halloween costume *and* I'd get to bare my belly.

These days, I would have a hard time putting together such an ensemble. I'll always have a soft spot for hot pink, but my wardrobe has more purple than pink. I'm still trying to figure out when I became a magenta girl and turned away from pastels. It seems unnatural. After all, most boys stick with their favorite color—blue—all their lives. Why do so many girls abandon pink? Is it because they no longer dream of (being) Jeannie, or is it because they're dreaming of something more?

Our Rosy Future

After years of living in the pink, we are now peering out at a rosy future. We have moved from crevasses to above treeline. If we were stuck in a crevasse or simply on the trail, you wouldn't be reading this book right now. Had we followed the good girl rules of publishing, this project would never have made it past the proposal stage.

In our pursuit of getting published, we had signed with two other agents before finding our current agent. Despite shopping the book to a dozen publishing houses, the first hotshot agent was not able to land us a deal. We're not even sure what the second agent did for us other than say we were the best thing since sliced bread. Surely there's something more remarkable than sliced bread that should replace this tired expression.

Being the aspiring bad girls that we are, we persevered. We found another agent who loved our work. We didn't mention our experience with the first agent for fear of losing the deal. (A *big* no-no in the publishing world.)

Our agent found out about the previous agent through the submissions process because an editor wrote and said, "I've already seen this proposal." Our second agent shot us a panicky email and we nearly slipped into good girl red alert—being plagued by guilt, engaging in self-flogging, apologizing endlessly, and trying to make everything all better. We called each other for bad girl support, took a collective deep breath, and did minimal damage control. Everybody lived, and a book was born.

The moral of the story: Sometimes you have to break the rules to get what you want.

ABOUT THE AUTHORS

Ann Tinkham is a writer based in Boulder, Colorado. She has written over thirty online courses in subjects ranging from emergency preparedness to energetic healing. Ann is working on a novel, *Analyzing Abbey*. Her fiction has appeared in *Apt, Edifice Wrecked, Hiss Quarterly, Lily, MotherVerse, Stone Table Review, Syntax, Thirst for Fire, Toasted Cheese*, and *Wild Violet*.

In addition to writing, Ann has talked her way out of an abduction and talked her way into the halls of the United Nations. She hitchhiked up a mountain in Switzerland, and worked her way down the corporate ladder.

———————————————

Carol Brunelli, a Boston native and Boulder, Colorado transplant, is a writer, dancer, and college administrator. She's written four books on US presidents for *Child's World*, and made her Hollywood début as a Lithuanian folk dancer in Lasse Hallströms' film *Once Around*.

Carol also speaks Spanish Madrileño style, writes for kids, and gets her groove on in the dance studio and in her living room. She is at home both in the foothills and in the concrete jungle. She's survived near-death experiences in the backcountry as well as Contra attacks in Nicaragua. Her advice for making love last is: once you get a foothold, secure your rope, and hold on tight.